Still  AROUND THE CLOCK

MARSHALL LYTLE

with MICHAEL JORDAN RUSH

Still ROCKIN' AROUND THE CLOCK

MY LIFE IN ROCK 'N' ROLL'S FIRST SUPERGROUP, THE ORIGINAL COMETS

AND

RECORDING THE SONG THAT MADE MUSIC HISTORY, "ROCK AROUND THE CLOCK"

MARSHALL LYTLE

with MICHAEL JORDAN RUSH

STILL ROCKIN' AROUND THE CLOCK

Published by Michael Jordan Rush
7801 Langdon Street, Terrace 1
Philadelphia, PA 19111-3565

ISBN: 1-4414-7780-2

All photos from the author's collection
Cover photos by Julie Marsella
Cover and layout by Karen Schwartz Design

First Edition

Printed in the United States of America

*I dedicate this book to my fans,
who have made it possible for me
to continue through the years
doing the job I love.*

*I've always believed that
if you're doing what you love,
you never have to work.*

Table of Contents

Foreword 1

The founding fathers of rock 'n' roll are now grandfathers and some even great grandfathers. For them, the legend lives on, and will continue to live on in the hearts and minds of many generations to come.

Marshall Lytle was one of Bill Haley's Comets. He was there at the very beginning, when a little cowboy band turned into the group that changed the way we think, dance and look. Marshall was a guitar player but learned to play slap bass from Bill Haley himself. He far exceeded Haley's expectations, so much so that his playing is now considered one of the sounds that define early rock 'n' roll.

Marshall doing some antics with bass fiddle in Europe

More important is that success has not changed the man. He has always lived life to the fullest and always been there for his family, friends and fans. He was there when Alan Freed was yelling "Rock 'n' roll everybody" over the microphone during his radio show. In the words of Marshall himself, "I want to rock 'til I drop."

Doing over 200 shows a year almost 60 years later is, as the title of the first rock song ever to enter the *Billboard* pop charts suggests, "Crazy Man Crazy." (Yes, that song was co-written by Bill Haley and Marshall Lytle.)

Jimmy Jay
**International Radio Personality
and Host of the *Rewind Show*
www.RewindShow.com**

Foreword 2

Rock Around the Clock and Me

I've often wondered if I'd never purchased a copy of Bill Haley and His Comets' "Thirteen Women (And Only One Man in Town)" in 1954 how the history of Rock and Roll might have changed. Of course, if my dad hadn't been Glenn Ford who was the star of the film *Blackboard Jungle* in which the flipside of that song was featured, it wouldn't have mattered. But I did, and he was, so I guess now the rest is just Rock and Roll history. This is my story. Rock on.

I began my writing exercise with MGM Studios' *Blackboard Jungle* in which my father starred as teacher Richard Dadier. I had a personal connection with the film and I thought it would be nice to detail that.

In my writing, I discussed the culture in postwar America before the production of Blackboard received at home and abroad when it was released in March 1955. I was also looking forward to telling a bit about my participation in how the theme song of the film, "(We're Gonna) Rock Around the Clock" (or "RATC") was discovered. However, in my research in the library and on the Internet, much to my amazement I discovered that there were already a few attributions, but I believed they were in error. Because of this, I decided to excerpt and expand upon this episode from my longer story about *Blackboard Jungle*.

Let me say at the onset, if anyone thinks they know how the song was chosen to be used in the film — they don't. This is how it really happened.

My parents were married in 1943 and each brought to the union their huge collections of record albums. My mother was dancer Eleanor Powell who starred in some of MGM's most endearing musicals, including the Broadway Melody series. Her taste in music reflected her show business background — swing and a little blues. Many of the era's greatest musical talents that she knew and worked with were guests in our home, from Arturo Toscanini to Tommy Dorsey. My father, meanwhile, had in his collection every imaginable record from every other musical discipline from symphonic to Hawaiian to Country. Their marriage was a merger of musical tastes and, happily, I was exposed to all of it. By age seven I could identify many classical compositions, knew many of the Big Band leaders and their work, and had developed an ardent interest in music. This eclectic education was definitely a defining element in my upbringing.

We had a room in our home in Beverly Hills, California, called the China Room. It was our music room and it was there we would often retire after dinner to enjoy whatever offering was on the evening's agenda. My mother would knit, my dad would study his scripts, and we would all listen to the record player.

My parents purchased this house from composer Max Steiner and the China Room had been his music room. Within in its walls he composed the scores of *Gone With the Wind, Casablanca,* and practically every film at Warner Brothers during Hollywood's Golden Age within its walls. It was the perfect place to hear music. There was an aura about that room, with its burnished gold leaf walls, deep red trim and door panels with Chinese figures painted in an oriental tableau. Today, I have many of those panels salvaged from a demolition crew working at the house after mom sold it. They are sacred to me because of the film history they had witnessed.

In the fall of 1954, I was a precocious

fifth grader who loved music. Between the Beverly Hills Music Shop and Wallich's Music City at Sunset and Vine, I was a busy lad indulging myself in the thing I loved most — my music. I loved rhythm and blues or "race music" as it was formally known in the late 1940s.

One of the records I bought during the fall of 1954 was "Thirteen Women (and Only One Man in Town)," recorded by a rockabilly group called Bill Haley and The Comets. Earlier I had purchased my first Haley record called "Crazy Man Crazy" and knew that this Haley fellow was on to something. I looked forward to their next release. When I brought "Thirteen Women" home and played it I didn't like it. As many kids did in those days, I turned the record over to discover the real A-side: "Rock Around the Clock." How Decca Records could have thought that "Thirteen Women" could have been the A-side was a mystery to me. Still, "RATC" sold well, rising to number 23 on the charts before the end of the year.

On October 4, 1954 my father was signed by MGM to star in what everyone felt was going to be a controversial film about a hot topic that was recently making news: juvenile delinquency. The film was called *Blackboard Jungle*. Pandro Berman was the producer and Richard Brooks was chosen to direct and write the screenplay from Evan Hunter's novel. Berman wanted to start production on the film immediately after he signed dad, as Hunter's book was scheduled to be serialized in the *Ladies' Home Journal* the same month. When the novel was published the previous August it caused quite a bit of controversy—so it was a "hot" property. But my father was already working on another project at the studio,

Peter Ford

Interrupted Melody, co-starring Eleanor Parker, so Berman had no choice but to wait for him. *Interrupted Melody* finished principal photography on Saturday, November 13, 1954. Shooting started two days later on *Blackboard Jungle.*

When I began my research to write an extensive article about the *Blackboard Jungle* and started investigating information about "RATC," I was quite delighted when the Internet provided me a wonderful and insightful tribute about the song and its history written by Alex Frazer-Harrison (www.rockabillyhall.com/RockClock-Tribute.html). This article had everything one would ever want to know about Bill Haley, his Comets, and the song "RATC." It had everything except one thing; like every other source I found, it misidentified how the song was "discovered" and eventually used in the picture. I contacted Alex, told him what I believed to be the true story, and he encouraged me to do further research to set the record straight.

There are many sources that concern the discovery of "RATC" as it applies to *Blackboard Jungle.* In some, including a biography of Bill Haley written by his son, John W. Haley and John Von Hoelle called *Sound and Glory,* it is stated that the song was first noticed by Richard Brooks, when he heard it playing on his daughter's record player. In other versions of the tale, Pandro Berman discovered "RATC" one day by hearing it playing on his daughter's record player. Both Brooks and Berman were deceased. I was determined to find their children to ask them if any of them had any direct involvement in "RATC" being used in *Blackboard Jungle.* I now know that none of them did.

Richard Brooks married Harriet Levin on

September 20, 1945. They had no children. I discovered that Richard and his second wife, actress Jean Simmons, who he married in 1960, did indeed have a daughter, Kate, but she wasn't born until July 9, 1961 — six years after *Blackboard Jungle* was made. So the association of "RATC" and the director's daughter was simply not possible. I now turned to the possibility that there could be a connection to the producer's daughter.

Bill Haley and The Comets recorded "Rock Around the Clock" on April 12, 1954 and the single was released in May. James E. Myers (a.k.a. Jimmy De Knight), who is credited with co-writing "RATC" with Max C. Freedman in 1953, said that after sales slowed on that record, he sent it to many producers in Hollywood, trying to generate renewed interest in the song. This could be true, but even if he did send it around, based on the films that Pandro Berman had produced until 1954 (Morning Glory, Follow the Fleet, National Velvet, and Ivanhoe to name just a few), it seems unlikely that he would have been interested in a song like "RATC." However, I knew I had to locate his children to make sure.

Berman had three children: Michael (b. 06/03/36), Susan (b. 12/01/41) and Cynthia (b. 07/13/42). I discussed the making of *Blackboard Jungle* and "RATC" with each of them. Michael remembered his dad telling him just before making the film, "You won't believe what's going on in the New York City school system. I'm going to do a film that will shock you." Later, Berman played "RATC" for his children. Michael asked, "Was this written expressly for the film?" His father answered, "No, this has been out, and it was a hit." The fact that his dad brought the record home (my copy I imagine) to play for his children was confirmed when Susan, Berman's eldest daughter said, "Dad came home with 'Rock Around the Clock' and played it for us. I loved it." So, it wasn't the son or at least one of Pandro's daughters who was playing "RATC" when he first heard the song. Berman brought it home and played it for them.

I now had to find the other daughter, and that took some doing. When I finally found Cynthia and asked her what she knew about how "Rock Around The Clock" got in the film, she answered, "the studio hired those two writers. You know Leiber and ...?" I said, "You mean Jerry Leiber and Mike Stoller?" She said "Yes, they're still around. They just sold their music rights recently. Call them. They'll tell you about it." Well, I had my answer. Leiber and Stoller were seminal composers and gave us much of early Rock and Roll's best music, but they had nothing to do with "RATC." I had now confirmed that it wasn't the director or the producer's daughters. It was my recording of "RATC" that Pandro Berman heard at his home.

Richard Brooks and my father would meet away from MGM during production to discuss the film. Working on a short schedule with no rehearsals with mainly non-actors was a test for everyone. Richard stopped by our house on occasion to visit dad and talk about the production. It was on one of these visits that Richard heard some records I owned. One of them was "Rock Around the Clock." I now know that he borrowed that record and some others on one of his visits.

Joel Freeman, who was the assistant director on *Blackboard Jungle,* recalled that toward the end of production, which would have been mid-December 1954, Brooks called him into his office to hear some records that he thought might possibly be used in the opening of the film. He played Joel three songs and they agreed that Haley's up-tempo "jump blues" tune was the perfect choice. I recently asked Joel what the other songs were but he didn't remember. My guess would be that in addition to "RATC" they could have been Big Joe Turner's version of "Shake Rattle and Roll" and quite possibly "All Night Long" by the Joe Houston Orchestra.

MGM eventually purchased the rights to "RATC" for $5,000 from Decca Records with the condition that they could only use the music three times in the film. It has been written that for $2,500 more they could have owned the song outright. The producer of Haley's recording, Milt Gabler, once claimed that MGM bought the song for a dollar.

Brooks, having found what he wanted,

would now also use the music in the beginning of the film over the opening credits as well as at the end. Since MGM had paid for another opportunity to use the song the music department at the studio cleverly used strains and riffs from "RATC" intermixed with some jazz music during the fight scene between Dadier and his fellow teacher Josh Edwards against the gang of juvenile delinquents who attacked them in an alley.

What I always knew and wanted to talk about before I began writing my article on *Blackboard Jungle* was my experience at first hearing "RATC" in the film. It was this memory that made me suspicious of all those other attributions that I discovered when I began my research. This is what happened:

As an early tenth birthday surprise, my father asked me if I'd like to go to the Encino Theatre in the San Fernando Valley to see *Blackboard Jungle*. It was Wednesday night

February 2, a night I'll never forget. It was the first showing of the film to the general public.

Dad knew that I would like it and told me to expect to hear "that song" somewhere during the film. All dad knew is that they laid in a music track for the first time and that "my song" was going to be in the film somewhere. We snuck into the back of the theatre along with Mr. Berman and Mr. Brooks just before it was to begin. The theater grew dark, and I remember very clearly my thoughts as the first scene opened on the empty blackboard as the credits rolled by: Wow! Not only were they playing "Rock Around the Clock," the song that dad had borrowed from my record collection and given to Mr. Brooks, but it was so loud — just like I played it at home. It was wonderful! I liked the film too, of course, but it was the music that I remember most. There couldn't have been a happier kid in the whole world than me at that moment.

"(We're Gonna) Rock Around the Clock" was the first rock song ever to be used in a motion picture. I recently asked Evan Hunter what he thought about "RATC" being used in the film. He said, "Terrific! It started the film off with a bang. Kids were getting up and dancing in the isles. Every kid in America went to see that film. They were carrying copies of the paperback book in the back pocket of their jeans." And dance they did, and caused some mischief too. Teenagers — misunderstood, lonely and rebellious — had discovered a touchstone with which they could identify. Teens at that time had been islands unto themselves, unaware that thousands of others were just like them. In celebrating "RATC," they became united, powerful and their spirit of unbridled freedom changed the culture of America forever.

By July 5, 1955, seven months after Richard Brooks first heard my 78 RPM copy of the record at my house, "RATC" was the top selling single in the nation. It stayed on the charts for eight weeks, eventually selling more than 25 million copies. After a good deal of research, I now feel that I can say with certainty that I played a small, but pivotal role in launching a musical revolution. Thanks to a unique set of circumstances, the musical passion of a 5th grader helped "RATC" become, as Dick Clark called it, "The National Anthem of Rock and Roll."

Peter Ford

www.PeterFord.com

Still ROCKIN' AROUND THE CLOCK

MARSHALL LYTLE

with MICHAEL JORDAN RUSH

Acknowledgments

I've had many requests from my fans over the years that I write my memoir. And now, as the clock winds down, I'm telling my story, to the best of my recollection.

I would like to express my love and gratitude to my mother and father and also to my sister and brothers — Clara, John Jr., nicknamed "High Pocket," Clifford, who is since deceased, and Gene, nicknamed "Influence," who looked after me and carried me on his back — literally — when I was unable to walk properly as a child due to a birth defect. Thank you all for putting up with me when I was growing up.

I would like to thank and express my love for all of my children: Marshall Jr., Larry, and Rodney who still live in the Pennsylvania area where they were born and grew up, and Jeffrey, Adam, Jason, Melissa and Ryan Bjaranson. And I am thankful to my former wives Marjorie Lytle and Sonja Bjaranson for raising the children to be such great citizens.

Thank you to all the guys in The Original Comets and especially my two partners, Joey Ambrose and Dick Richards, with whom I've been friends and worked for almost sixty years.

I would also like to thank our current Comets of the last few years, David Byrd on piano and Jackson Haney on guitar. We hope you're with us forever.

Thank you to all the people I've worked with in show business. I appreciate your friendship and good wishes, and hope to be associated with you for a long time to come.

Thank you to everyone who assisted with this book,

Marshall in a 1954 photo of
Bill Haley and His Comets

including my niece, Gail (known as Shayna Golda), Jay Katz, Esq., Andrew Stein, Esq., Jimmy Jay and Peter Ford.

I want to thank the publisher of this book, Mr. Michael Jordan Rush, for believing in me enough to put this book on the market and make it available for you wonderful people to ponder through. Maybe you will keep it as a reminder of the early days of rock 'n' roll and let your youngsters and favorite people in your life read it. Some of it is history.

And finally, thank you to Cathy Smith, the love of my life, who loves me for who I am and not just as an entertainer.

— *Marshall Lytle*

Introduction

I am Marshall Lytle, a proud member of the Rockabilly Hall of Fame. In spite of that distinction, if I were a betting man, I would wager almost anything that virtually nobody other than my loyal fans, circle of friends and my family has any idea of who I am.

I would also wager, however, that anybody with even just a passing appreciation of rock 'n' roll is familiar with the ground-breaking legacy of which I was a part and am still intimately involved.

You see, I was an original member of Bill Haley and His Comets and part of the making, recording and playing of "Rock Around the Clock," the signature song that launched rock 'n' roll into the musical universe.

You might say that since the release of "Rock Around the Clock," the music world as we know it changed forever and the whole world has been rocking and rolling around the clock, 24/7, ever since.

The original Bill Haley and The Comets truly earned the title of the First Band of Rock 'n' Roll. On April 12, 1954, ten years before The Beatles landed in New York, the original Bill Haley and His Comets went into Decca Records' New York City recording studio and, in thirty minutes and two takes, recorded the song that launched rock 'n' roll. Listed in *Guinness World Records,* "Rock Around the Clock" became the best-selling single by a group. I was amazed when James Myers, co-writer of the song, told me that it has sold 80 million copies! And it sounds as good today as it did the day we recorded it. Dick Clark has called it "the National Anthem of Rock 'n' Roll."

I was there from the earliest days of Bill Haley and The Comets (and even before, when we were still Bill Haley and The Saddlemen) through the recording of our two biggest singles, "Rock Around the Clock" and "Shake, Rattle and Roll," when we were sitting on top of the music world.

I feel so lucky to be doing what I love for much of the past 60 years. Come take an amazing ride with me through these pages recalling my life in rock 'n' roll and the story of recording "Rock Around the Clock," the song that made music history.

Still ROCKIN'
AROUND THE CLOCK

While "Rock the Joint" was playing,
Alan (Freed) got really excited.
He turned the microphone switch on
and kept yelling, "Rock 'n' roll everybody!
Rock 'n' roll!"

After the record played,
the telephone started ringing off the hook.
People kept calling up and saying
"Play that rock 'n' roll song again."
He played the song 12 times that one night.

And it was in that studio and on that night,
in the spring of 1952, that I truly believe
"rock 'n' roll" was born.

Bill Haley and The Saddlemen

I was born in 1933, during the Depression years, in the small town of Old Fort, at the foothills of the mountains in North Carolina, just down from Asheville.

We had a very poor upbringing. My parents had nothing. There were five children in our family. My sister, the first born, was named Clara Belle Lytle. Then came John Lytle Jr., named after my father John Lytle Sr. The third child was Clifford Lytle, now deceased. The fourth was Gene Lytle. And I was the baby of five children.

I was born with a birth defect — I had club feet. My mother wanted me to have surgery. My father didn't because of, I guess, money reasons, as in we didn't have any. My mother wouldn't take that for an answer,

Marshall at six years old

and she got a hold of the Shriners organization. They put me in their hospital at about the age of six months. I had an operation on my feet which straightened them from being turned inward to a straight line. The operation was very good but at about the age of six years I jumped off of a porch or something and I damaged them again.

I had to go back into the hospital for additional surgery. I had three major operations altogether on my feet and finally my feet were corrected. I'm so thankful to my mother for having that done. Otherwise I would not have walked properly.

I had a pretty normal childhood. I went

to school in North Carolina up to the fourth grade. That was in the beginning of World War II. My older brothers, Johnny and Clifford, enlisted in the Navy. That left my brother Gene and me at home.

My sister Clara had married and moved north to Pennsylvania into the town of Chester, near Philadelphia. Her husband was also in the military, in the Army, and Clara was trying to raise a family. She told my mother there was economic opportunity up there in Pennsylvania.

My father went to Chester, and then sent for his family. We got on a train in North Carolina and choo choo'ed up to Chester in the year of 1942. My mother went to work at the Sun Shipbuilding and Dry Dock Company. Not long after, my parents got divorced and my mother raised us.

My brother Gene and I went to school. Our family didn't have much, but those were still good times for us. We lived in a housing project out in Upland, Pennsylvania. The winters were a lot of fun, with sledding up and down the hills. We had a lot of snow back then.

Gene Lytle and Marshall, 2008

When the war was over, my brothers Clifford and Johnny came home from the Navy and got jobs. Then Johnny got married.

My brother Clifford was the one in our family with musical talent. He sang country and western music because from childhood we had been listening to the *Grand Ole Opry,* our favorite radio program. It was a clear channeled radio station that we could get not only in North Carolina but also when we got to Pennsylvania.

We went to nearby entertainment parks that brought in country and western stars. One was called Sunset Park, out near Avondale, Pennsylvania. They used to bring in Tex Ritter, Roy Acuff, and Ernest Tubb and the Texas Troubadours. All the big stars from the *Grand Ole Opry* came to

Sunset Park and played. We went to see them and enjoyed them.

Bill Haley came into our lives. Around 1947 Bill had a band out of Chester, Pennsylvania called Bill Haley and the Four Aces of Western Swing. He was running a place called Radio Park. These were the days before television, and people would bring a picnic lunch and sit with friends and watch a show.

Bill Haley, 1947

The shows were created by a promoter named Cousin Lee. Bill Haley became associated with Cousin Lee, who turned Radio Park over to Bill. They would pay some acts, and then there were free acts like myself getting up to sing.

One of Bill Haley's musicians, Tex King,

became very close with my brother Clifford. Cliff brought him home. Tex was looking for an inexpensive place to stay, so my mother rented him a room in our home.

Tex used to sit around our house playing the guitar and rehearsing songs. I became quite attached to his singing and playing. I would grab the old family guitar and go in my room and learn some of the songs Tex had played in Bill Haley's band. I learned new tunes, like songs from Eddy Arnold and other singers we admired. We bought records, which were pretty inexpensive back then, and I learned songs right off of the records.

Clifford was trying to get started in show business and would go down and sit in with Bill Haley, and Bill would always get him up to sing. Clifford played guitar and sang, but he had a regular job and didn't go on to become a professional entertainer.

Bill would always find people who were

just starting out in show business, and he'd get them up to sing a song, just to help them out a little bit.

Because his guitarist lived at our home, Bill Haley used to come over. My mother would make breakfast for him and he became a family friend.

As the years progressed, I started to become really interested in show business. I'd learn songs and sit on the steps and the girls would gather around and I would sing to them. Then I'd sing in some school assemblies.

My mother got me involved in some amateur shows. There were a lot of talent shows presented in those days. I remember when I was 16 years old I did the Paul

1950, Marshall at 17 years old

Whiteman talent show out of Philadelphia. I sang and played my guitar. I did "I'm Just a Plain Old Country Boy," a country song recorded by Jimmy Dickens from the *Grand Ole Opry.*

I didn't win the talent show but a very wonderful, tremendously talented lady by the name of Diane Carroll did. The Paul Whiteman show was a network show on WFIL television in Philadelphia, and it went all across America. It got me more interested in show business and I did a lot of other local shows around the Philadelphia area.

Before long, I was able to get my own radio show. It was a small 1000-watt station in Chester, Pennsylvania called WVCH that broadcast throughout the Delaware Valley. I got an offer to do a 15-minute radio show at 7:15 AM, just singing and playing my guitar and doing requests.

Bill Haley had himself been broadcasting

on a local radio
station by the
call letters
WPWA, located
in Brookhaven,
Pennsylvania
just outside of
Chester.

Dick Thomas, who had a hit
record in 1949 called "Sioux
City Sue," and Marshall, on
Chester, Pennsylvania radio

One day back
in 1951, Bill Haley came by WVCH where I
was doing my radio program. He said, "Hey
Marshall, my bass player just quit. Why
don't you come and be my bass player?"

I said, "Oh, Bill, I don't know how to
play the bass. I play the guitar and sing."
He said "Well, hey, that's not a difficult
thing to learn. I can teach you how to play
that thing in about half an hour." I said,
"Well, you know, let me try it."

So we went over to his radio station,
WPWA where he had an old bass fiddle
sitting out. He showed me the basics of
how to slap the bass fiddle and slap with a
shuffle beat: ba-doomba-doomba-doomba-

doomba; doomba-doomba-doomba-doo. That's what he wanted me to learn. So he showed me the basic notes that went with that beat.

I said, "Hell, I can do that." I went and bought a bass fiddle that afternoon in South Philadelphia and went to work for him that night over at a place called the Twin Bar in Gloucester, New Jersey. That was in the fall of 1951. I had just turned 18.

That was the start of my professional music career. I actually had a steady job! The three of us — Billy Williamson and Johnny Grande and me — each made $60 a week, and Bill Haley made $90 a week.

We did a matinee on Sunday afternoons from 3 to 5 PM or something like that. At nights we played from 9 PM until 2 AM. The Twin Bar was two semi-circular bars joined together and we played in the middle.

We had no fixed sets at all. We just called off the songs as we wanted to do them. We didn't have a list. We just wanted to do as many songs as we could, because we had to fill up the time.

We did six nights a week and we did a one hour radio program every day. I gave up my WVCH radio show because I had become one of Bill Haley's band members.

In the meantime, Bill's band had changed its name from The Four Aces of Western Swing to Bill Haley and The Saddlemen. So I became a Saddleman. We wore cowboy clothes and boots and hats at the beginning of our careers. That was in late 1951. With six days a week, five shows a night, 45 minutes on and 15 minutes off, we had to do a lot of songs. We played a lot of music.

There were just four of us in the band. Bill was the leader. Then there was Johnny Grande who played the accordion, Billy Williamson who played the steel guitar, and me on the bass fiddle. We had no drums in the band.

Bill played guitar and I played bass. That was our rhythm section. And Bill wanted it loud. During some of the songs he would yell over, "Play it louder Marshall, play it louder." I didn't have an amplifier in those days. It was long before electric basses were invented.

So I had to pull the strings and just grit my teeth. I got blood blisters on my fingers from pulling on the strings and I'd splatter blood all over the side of my bass and just keep going. Pretty soon I developed some very good calluses on my fingers.

Bill Haley played bass himself and during our sets, when I would sing a song, Bill would play the bass fiddle and I would play the guitar. I would probably sing five or six songs and Bill would sing eight or ten songs and we'd play a few instrumentals to fill in the time.

Bill Haley (playing bass), Johnny, Marshall, Billy

We didn't have rehearsed arrangements on

our songs. When we sang it was all "head arrangements" and all we'd do is tell the other guys, "it's in the key of G guys, let's go at it." One would start and the rest of us would play. And it was fun because we all had good ears. We heard the chords and we knew the sounds that needed to be played. We created our own arrangements as we worked.

We all would learn a new song together. Sometimes I even learned a new song by putting nickels in a jukebox and writing down the words as the guy sang them and it cost me maybe fifty cents in nickels to get all the lyrics off of a record from a jukebox. Then I would go and sing the song in the show. It was usually a big, popular song that everybody knew and enjoyed.

Because $60 a week wasn't much income even in those days, and because to get to the Twin Bar it was necessary to travel on the Chester ferry across the Delaware River, and then drive about 20-30 miles up to Paulsboro and Gloucester, New Jersey, Bill Haley and I used to ride together — either in Bill's '49 Plymouth or my '49 Ford.

Bill Haley, John Grande, Billy Williamson and Marshall on July 6, 1952, Bill's 27th birthday

So, on many occasions, we would meet Billy Williamson and Johnny Grande at the Chester ferry, and the four of us would all ride to work together. Coming home at two or three o'clock in the morning, we would usually stop at a little roadside diner. I'll never forget that. It was just like a little truck stop on the main highway going up to Gloucester, New Jersey.

Bill Haley's favorite sandwich was turkey with mayonnaise. I got to really enjoy that too because the cook at this diner would cook a fresh turkey every day and the meat was not processed meat; it was right off of a freshly-cooked turkey. Boy it was good! Probably didn't cost but 50 cents or something like that back then. The Saddlemen also played

September 1, 1952
Marshall's 19th birthday at
the Shelter Haven Hotel

the Shelter Haven Hotel in Stone Harbor on my 19th birthday.

Bill Haley was married and having problems with his first wife Dorothy. He would confide in me about his family problems. Then he met a pretty girl at the Twin Bar. Before I realized it, they had struck up quite a relationship.

Her name was Barbara Joan Cupcek and she had a nickname, "Cuppy." On November 14, 1952, Bill and Dorothy got divorced. Just four days later, on November 18, Bill married Cuppy and they started a family.

In 1952, there was a disc jockey at WPWA doing a rhythm and blues show called "Judge Rhythm's Court." His name was "Shorty the Bailiff." His real name was James Reeves.

One day he came to Bill and said, "Bill, there's a great song here recorded by Jimmy Preston. Boy it's really popular. It's called "Rock the Joint." Bill got a copy of it and learned it.

We started performing it at the Twin Bar. The crowds just went crazy over it because we played a rhythm and blues song with a country and western band. Bill said, "Boy, we're gonna record that song."

And record it we did, on Essex Records in the spring of 1952. It became very popular.

2007 – Marshall at a plaque on the wall of The Twin Bar for the 55th anniversary of "Rock the Joint" performances there by The Saddlemen

David Miller, the owner of Essex Records, really captured our unique rhythm section sound, with the slap bass serving as the rhythm section and no drums in the band.

The band's guitar sound enjoyed a major upgrade courtesy of the fantastic Danny Cedrone from Philadelphia, who had a band of his own called The Esquire Boys. He played on most all of Bill Haley's recordings up until "Shake, Rattle and Roll." Danny had a wonderful feel for playing the type of music that Bill and our band played.

When "Rock the Joint" was finished and started making a little noise in the music world, Dave Miller had our band go to Cleveland, Ohio to do a show and a radio interview on WJW with a new disc jockey named Alan Freed who played "black music," commonly referred to as rhythm and blues.

Alan was known in the Cleveland area as "The King of the Moondogs." He really liked our recording of "Rock the Joint," and he played it on his *Moondog* radio show during our interview, at about midnight.

We had gathered around this big old table with a boom microphone out in the middle of the table. Alan Freed had a wall switch that turned the microphones on and off. While "Rock the Joint" was playing, Alan got really excited. He turned the microphone switch on and kept yelling, "Rock 'n' roll everybody! Rock 'n' roll!"

After the record played, the telephone started ringing off the hook. People kept calling up and saying "Play that rock 'n' roll song again." Alan played the song again, and he played it again and again, and he kept yelling "Rock 'n' roll everybody!" each time the record played. He played the song 12 times that one night. And it was in that studio and on that night, in the spring of 1952, that I truly believe "rock 'n' roll" was born.

We started getting interested in recording other songs. When promoting "Rock the Joint," we wanted to find out what the kids thought of our music, so we would do a lot of high school assemblies.

One day, in Eddystone, Pennsylvania, we performed at an assembly just before lunch. Bill and I had ridden to the school together, and after the show was over and we were putting the instruments — my bass and his guitar — back in his car, the kids gathered around us.

Bill said, "Hey, what did you think of our music?" One kid said, "That's crazy, man, crazy." Bill took a pen and he wrote "crazy man crazy" on his hand. We thanked all the kids for enjoying our music and left. We went back to Bill's apartment which was not too far away.

While Cuppy was making us lunch, Bill grabbed a guitar. He struck a chord and said "Crazy, man, crazy. Crazy, man, crazy. Crazy, man, crazy. Man that music's gone, gone."

Then we started throwing lines back and forth. I would come up with a line and Bill would use it, and then he would come up with a line and use it. Bill and I basically wrote "Crazy Man Crazy," our next big hit, in about 30 minutes right there in his kitchen.

When we recorded "Crazy Man Crazy" on Essex Records, Dave Miller decided we should record it in New York City. Dave was basically responsible for creating the clickety-click sound that Bill Haley became known for. Dave decided to add drums to the band, so he hired a session drummer who had played music with a lot of different bands and orchestras. His name was Billy Gussack. He had been on the Arthur Godfrey show with Archie Bleyer's Orchestra, which also played on *Your Show of Shows* with Sid Caesar. He was a marvelous, marvelous drummer.

> "Crazy Man Crazy"…turned out
> to be our first big hit record
> and was the first rock 'n' roll song
> that ever hit the *Billboard* charts

Billy started playing around what I played, and putting in his little fills and things like that. We came up with a rhythm sound that was very infectious. On "Crazy Man Crazy'" that rhythm section just clicked. It really made people want to dance. I suppose Billy and I created our sound with "Crazy Man Crazy." That sound gelled immediately. It was the sound we took later to "Rock Around the Clock." It was the signature rhythm to which everybody liked to dance.

After the record was finished, I was standing by when Dave Miller asked Bill Haley, "Who's the writers on this, Bill?" And Bill said, "just Bill Haley."

And I went over to him and I said, "Bill, now you know that you and I wrote that song together." And Bill said, "Oh I know that Marshall, but I just want to take credit on this one by myself." He said, "I'll take care of you on some other songs."

Bill Haley was my hero in those days and I totally trusted him. I said, "OK, Bill." So Bill Haley's name was put on "Crazy Man Crazy," which really, basically, turned out to be our first big hit record and was the first rock 'n' roll song that ever hit the *Billboard* charts, and received a lot of attention in the record world.

But after a while, I started to feel Bill had taken advantage of me, and I started wondering about our relationship.

In the spring of '52, back at WPWA, a gentleman entered into the life of Bill Haley and The Saddlemen. His name was Lord Jim Ferguson.

Jim Ferguson was a WPWA radio host. He would go to local restaurants and talk to the owner and tell the owner that in exchange for free food and X amount of money, he would talk about the restaurant on the radio and put it in his newsletter.

Bill Haley and Marshall
Stone Harbor, New Jersey
1952

Because Jim and Bill and The Saddlemen

each had radio shows on WPWA, we all became friends. Jim told Bill Haley that he wanted to become the band's manager.

They created a partnership between Bill Haley, Billy Williamson, Johnny Grande and Jim Ferguson. And they left me out. I went right into the middle of the conversation and I said, "Hey, what about me?" And Bill Haley

Hanging out with some friends
The Saddlemen, 1952

said, "Oh, Marshall, you're gonna be a junior partner with us." So I said, "OK Bill, you'll take care of me." He said "Yeah, we're gonna take care of you, man. You're gonna make more money than you ever saw."

So being just 19 years old and still totally inexperienced in the business world, I once again put my trust and faith in my hero, Bill Haley.

After we recorded "Crazy Man Crazy" with drums, and that partnership was created, with me as a junior partner, we all decided we needed a drummer in the band. We had tried out a couple of drummers like Billy Gussack who just came and sat in with us one time.

The very first drummer who ever played with Bill Haley was named Earl Famous, but he couldn't meet our needs because of job commitments or something.

So we hired a young drummer from Eddystone, Pennsylvania by the name of Charlie Higler. He was 16 years old when he joined us. After Charlie was with us about six months, his father insisted that Charlie should be a partner in the band. That was all Bill needed to know. They decided to let him go and have a different drummer.

Charlie now lives down in Florida. I met up with him a couple of years ago when we were on a cruise. Charlie had a career in the real estate world. He's now living retired down in Florida, having a great time.

In 1953 we hired a drummer named Dick Richards, who became the basic first full-time drummer, who stayed with The Comets for years until 1955.

We continued to record but Bill was a stubborn guy. He thought that because Billy Gussack played drums on "Crazy Man Crazy" and did such a great job, that he was Bill's good luck charm. So when we recorded, Billy Gussack was the drummer on most of the recordings. Panama Francis was the drummer on "Shake, Rattle and Roll."

But Dick was still there, present in the studio. Sometimes he played the cow bell, and sometimes he played introductions on some of the songs like "Birth of the Boogie." Dick never really got to be the record-playing drummer. But he was always the band-playing drummer.

Marshall's house that he bought in 1952
for $5,000 and lived in until 1958

We worked hard but also had a lot of fun together. We all used to enjoy fishing. The first boat that Bill Haley owned was called "The Comets." We had it in Stone Harbor, New Jersey. Bill and I used to go shark fishing all the time. This was in 1952 or '53. We'd take that little boat out and we'd see what we could catch but we caught a lot of little sharks and we'd throw them back. We used to break down a lot in that little boat because Bill was not much of a mechanic and neither was I, especially at fixing boats.

On several occasions, when the engine died and we didn't know what to do, somebody would hook a rope on us and tow us back to the dock.

One day, we had gone on a fishing expedition with all The Saddlemen – Bill Haley, Billy Williamson, Johnny Grande and me and Jim Ferguson. The owner of the boat was Marty Hahn, and it was about a 28 foot cabin cruiser. We went from Stone Harbor out into the Atlantic, and we were out in deep water. We had a big old shark hook and we caught some fish that

Marshall with his 1941 Lincoln Zephyr

Wildwood, New Jersey, late 1952

we didn't want to eat so we used the fish for bait and we hung it off the back of that boat.

We caught a big shark that was maybe eight feet long. We gutted it and brought it on board and we took that fish over to Wildwood, New Jersey where we were performing at the HofBrau Hotel. The HofBrau was our favorite place to play in Wildwood.

We had Harry Broomall, who was our roadie – they used to call him "Red" Broomall because he had flaming red hair – and we had him build a scaffolding off of the second level of the HofBrau Hotel and we hoisted that big shark right up off of the sidewalk, and people gathered around and it created quite a lot of commotion and talk among the patrons. We left it there for a day and pretty soon it started having quite an odor so we had to take it down because I think the police came over and said you've got to remove that thing. It smelled just awful.

Bill generally didn't hang out with the rest of the guys. Even right after I first joined his band, he became kind of a private person. All the rest of us hung out together and we drank together and did all kinds of stuff, but Bill was a little bit standoffish, even with his fans. He was not a people person.

Bill was a great speaker because he had the radio experience and he spoke very well, but he got to a point where he just didn't want to go and visit people and do radio interviews and things like that. I remember him asking Dick Richards and me, "You guys go over here to this radio station and do an interview with such and such a disc jockey." And we did that several times.

When I first went with the band I used to go out to Bill's house all the time in Booth's Corner, Pennsylvania when he lived in a converted chicken coup; that's what some people called it. But I think his father had originally converted an old shack of some sort, where maybe the chickens stayed at one time, but it was a nice little house. Bill and Cuppy had gotten married and after we started having some success and the royalties started rolling in, I guess this was about in 1954, Bill was getting ready to build Melody Manor which was his house out there on the balance of the five acres. There were some trees and things in the way and I went out there and helped him cut them down and we pulled up stumps with trucks and just getting it ready for contractors to come in and build his house.

It's still there. I visited the house in the early 80s and I talked to the new owners of the house, and they were very gracious. One of the owners invited me into the house and I had told her that this is the home where we rehearsed "Rock Around the Clock" in the basement and so on and so forth and she wasn't aware of the history of the house they owned.

She got a big picture that had been left in the attic of the house. She asked me who was in the photograph and I said that it's Bill Haley's father holding Bill as a baby when he was six months old. And that photograph is in the front of the book called *Sound and Glory,* written by Jack Haley, Bill's first born son.

We had to haul our instruments around and the bass fiddle was always a kind of a pain in the neck because of its size. I had bought a car, a 1951 Nash Ambassador that I could fit the bass in the back seat with the neck of the bass up in the back window and I didn't have to have the neck hanging over the front seat. That was kind of a neat thing for hauling the bass. It was kind of a fun car to drive, too.

"Rock Around the Clock"
went to number one and became
the first number one rock 'n' roll song
in the United States.

Listed in *Guinness World Records,*
"Rock Around the Clock" became the
best-selling single by a group.
I was amazed when James Myers,
co-writer of the song, told me
that it has sold 80 million copies!

Dick Clark has called
"Rock Around the Clock"
"the National Anthem of Rock 'n' Roll."

Bill Haley and The Comets

We became The Comets in late '52 after Lord Jim Ferguson had come into the lives of Bill Haley and The Comets. We were still Bill Haley and the Saddlemen when that partnership was created.

Bill had a live radio program on WPWA from 12 noon to 1 PM. We were hanging around the lobby and the station's program director, Bob Johnson, came out of his office and said, "Hey, you guys ought to change your names. You don't look like Saddlemen. You really should change your name to Haley's Comets because of that comet that flies across the sky, called Halley's Comet. You could associate yourself with that comet."

So we thought about it and Bill Haley said "What do you guys think of that? Haley's Comets." I said, "That's a great idea. That's a great name for a band, Haley's Comets." Johnny and Billy thought so too.

So we took the cowboy clothes off, put on suits and bow ties and we became Bill Haley's Comets. We played the same music we did

The early Comets, 1953

as the Saddlemen but we started switching over and playing more rhythm and blues in our shows. And when we added the drums, it gave us another flavor that we didn't have as a four-piece country and western band.

Then, on one of our recording sessions, Dave Miller hired a saxophone player which gave us even more of a rhythm and blues sound. Right after that session, the band decided we needed to hire a saxophone. And a young lad named Joey D'Ambrosio auditioned. Bill gave him the name of Joey Ambrose because D'Ambrosio was difficult for him to pronounce. So Joey Ambrose the saxophone player became Joey Ambrose the Comet. He passed the audition. He was just a young lad of 18 when he came with the band.

Our sound really came to life when we added the voicing of Joey's saxophone to the guitar and the steel guitar, because the sax would play the riffs with the guitars and give it all a sound like a big band. Adding the saxophone was a major part of creating the Bill Haley sound that became famous around the world.

I was often known for my antics with the bass. It started in Wildwood, New Jersey in 1953 on a Sunday afternoon. We had 3-400 people, some in their bathing suits, some in their shorts, very casual, and everyone was having a great time. We were playing early rock 'n' roll music, and our saxophone player, Joey, was kind of new with the band at that particular time. We were doing a saxophone instrumental, "Night Train" or some crazy song, and he decided that he would go out into the audience and honk at some of the customers. Then he stood up on a table and played and I said, "Oh boy, I think I gotta get in on this, because it's really exciting."

So I put the bass in an angled position and I stood on it, and I was playing and the audience went nuts! And then I said, "Wow they really liked that, I wonder if I can do something else." So I threw it up over my head and played it over my head. And they liked that too and they just went crazy over it. And then I said, "Well, let me see what else I can do with this crazy thing." So I laid it on the stage and I lay down on top of it. And Joey came over and he threw his leg over top of me and he was riding my back like a horse. The audience was really enjoying it. So I turned the bass over on its other side and I said, "Joe, sit down here on the bass." And I slid him across the floor, and

Marshall performing bass antics at a recent performance

he was honking and he had his feet up in the air and I was sliding him around in circles, and the audience really enjoyed that. Every time we would do something like that the applause would be thunderous.

We just kept trying to do different things. I would spin the bass around and catch it in strange ways. I turned it upside down and played it with the bottom up. Sometimes I held it like a guitar.

I still do the bass antics in our shows. The bass weighs about 30 pounds. It's a good workout. The exercise that I get during an hour-and-a-half show is pretty good, so I don't have to go to the gym every day. So that's what we started in 1953 and it just continued on through our whole lives.

We did the antics in the movies and bass players around the world saw us play. When we went back to England in 1989 for a reunion show, there were dozens and dozens of bass players there just to see me and pay homage to me.

When Joey and Dick were hired with the band, they kind of looped me into the sideman category and Joe and Dick and I became equals. My "junior partnership" had gone right out the window. Now I was just a hired hand. My feelings of Bill Haley as my hero started turning to feelings of Bill Haley the jerk. I never showed any of those feelings, but inside I grew tired of Bill and all his promises that were never fulfilled.

Years later, Bill's wife Cuppy told me Bill was very jealous of me even back in the Twin Bar days, because he thought I was singing directly to her when I was doing love songs. The truth is, I would just look at the women and sing to everybody. I didn't know it at the time, but Bill had a jealous streak in him about me and my talents.

As the years progressed and the hit records started coming, we signed a recording contract with Decca Records. Our first recording session was scheduled for April 12, 1954. We were to record a song we had never heard of called "Thirteen Women and Only One Man in Town." On the flip side we planned to record "Rock Around the Clock."

We had a problem getting to New York City that day. We were on a ferry crossing the Delaware River from Chester, from where we would then get on the New Jersey Turnpike and head to New York for the session. The ferry boat got caught on a sandbar.

Bill Haley took the delay in stride. He knew Milt Gabler at Decca Records would understand. Gabler was, by the way, the uncle of comedian Billy Crystal. "So what if we're a little late?" Bill said. "They'll get us off this sandbar and we'll be in the studio before you know it."

With the help of a rising tide, a tug boat came over to pull us, and helped get the ferry boat back to the dock. Then we had to transfer our instruments and things so we could get off the ferry and get to our recording session in New York City.

We were about two hours late in arriving, and Decca Records was very upset and there was a lot of tension. This was our first recording session for Decca, and because Sammy Davis Jr. was scheduled to record after we were through, we couldn't go over time. Milt gave us three hours.

When we arrived at the Pythian Temple, Decca's recording studio, they gave us a piece of music and said this is what we're going to record and it was called "Thirteen Women and Only One Man in Town."

Since we'd never even heard of the song, we had to completely learn it and create an arrangement on the spot. It took us two and a half hours to record "Thirteen Women" and get it in the can.

After "Thirteen Women" was finished, Milt Gabler, who was Decca's head of Artists and Repertoire, said "OK, now you guys can do that rock thing that you're gonna do."

One of the co-writers of "Rock Around the Clock," James Myers, actually got us the recording contract for Decca Records. As repayment, Bill said that he would record "Rock Around the Clock."

We had rehearsed "Rock Around the Clock" the night before in Bill's basement in Boothwyn, Pennsylvania. That was the first time we had ever played it.

At the rehearsal were Bill, Johnny Grande, Joey Ambrose, Billy Williamson, Dick Richards and me. We created the arrangement we wanted to do on "Rock Around the Clock." Danny Cedrone, who played guitar, was not at that rehearsal but showed up at the recording session.

After we finished recording "Thirteen Women," we went over the song once and Danny Cedrone was looking for a guitar solo to play because Bill wanted one on almost all of the recordings. Danny was fooling around for something to play, and we had only 30 minutes to record "Rock Around the Clock."

About ten minutes in, I said, "Danny, why don't you play that great guitar solo you played on 'Rock the Joint' a couple of years ago?" And he said, "You think that would fit here?" And I said, "Yeah, let's try it." So we played it again and Danny did this guitar solo and it worked so very, very well on "Rock Around the Clock." It fit perfectly and it became one of the greatest guitar solos ever.

We did two takes of "Rock Around the Clock" and ran out of time. The engineer, with those two takes, took Bill's voice out of one and put it in the other and created the master. And that's the song that became world famous.

People have asked me if we thought "Rock Around the Clock" was going to be the world-wide hit it became. To tell the truth, I thought "Rock Around the Clock" was a good song, but it was not something we had great enthusiasm about. We always had hopes for a hit record, but we never realized "Rock Around the Clock" would be world famous. You couldn't sense it.

I feel rock 'n' roll was born before "Rock Around the Clock." But they were merely stepping stones to what "Rock Around the Clock" achieved.

I received a union scale paycheck of $41.25. That was what I earned for my part on one of the world's most famous recordings.

It sold about 150,000 copies initially but got new life the following year when director Richard Brooks used it in the soundtrack to the movie *Blackboard Jungle*. The song came to Brooks' attention from Peter Ford, son of the star of that movie, Glenn Ford. In July of 1955, "Rock Around the Clock" went to number one and became the first number one rock 'n' roll song in the United States. Decca had reissued "Rock Around the Clock" in April 1955 with "Rock Around the Clock" as the A side and it was number one on the *Billboard* charts for eight weeks.

In June 1954, right after we recorded "Rock Around the Clock" and "Thirteen Women," Decca had us come back to the studio and record "Shake, Rattle and Roll." "ABC Boogie" was on the other side of it.

"Shake, Rattle and Roll" became a big hit for us. We were touring and promoting it when it

Our first gold record dinner –
Decca Records sold one million copies
of "Shake, Rattle and Roll"

entered the charts in July 1954 and reached number four in December 1954. Decca gave us a gold record for "Shake, Rattle and Roll" which they presented to us at a dinner.

1954 was a big year for us touring the United States. We went to Reno and Las Vegas and played a lot of big shows because we were a headline act thanks to "Shake, Rattle and Roll."

On a sad note, Danny Cedrone died in a fall just two weeks after he recorded "Shake, Rattle and Roll" with us. Danny was very well thought of. His guitar is in the Rock and Roll Hall of Fame in Cleveland, Ohio.

I recall being at Universal Studios in Hollywood and doing Bill Haley's first film, *The Roundup of Rhythm*. We were a pretty popular act at that time. It was a motion picture short and didn't even feature "Rock Around the Clock" because it had not yet become a hit.

We did "Shake, Rattle and Roll," "Crazy Man Crazy," and "Straight Jacket." That's the film where I did the antics, standing on the bass, sliding Joey around the floor, and that type of thing.

I remember Tony Curtis and Janet Leigh met us in the parking lot at Universal and invited us to come to their house because they were really big fans of our music. We had to decline because we had other commitments for interviews and shows and things like that, but it was sure nice to have been invited.

Another cute little thing happened when my first wife Marjorie and I were driving around Beverly Hills looking at where all the beautiful movie stars lived. We pulled up to a stoplight and a movie star pulled up alongside. It was Gregory Peck. I knew that Marjorie really loved this guy.

I said "Honey, of all the people here in Hollywood, who would be the one you'd most like to see?" And she said, "Oh, you know I'd love to see Gregory Peck." And I said "Well, if you turn your head to the right you'll see him because he's only six feet from you right now in the car next door to you." She turned her head and she saw him and, oh, she was just so pleased about that.

When we were filming at Universal Studios, it was a great joy to go into the commissary for lunch and look around and see all the movie stars we had admired for many, many years. Bing Crosby, Gregory Peck, Burt Lancaster, and all the other major, major stars were just there having lunch.

For us old country boys who were creating rock 'n' roll, that was a big deal. I was star struck, and I still am today to a certain degree. I love being around people who have made it big in show business, and yet when I look at myself I kind of forget that I made it too, having played a big part in creating this tremendous music that people have enjoyed for the last 55 years.

Bill bought a touring vehicle for the group to use. It was almost like a delivery truck, not overly large but about a half ton panel truck.

Bill bought that in 1954, I believe, when we started to tour. It was a Ford panel truck and we had "Decca Records" and "Bill Haley and the Comets" painted on the side of it. Harry Broomall was in charge of our instruments and was responsible for setting them up and taking our uniforms to the cleaners and making sure that everything was prim and proper.

It was very good after we got the panel truck because it took a big load off of our

1954 when The Comets headlined at the Steel Pier in Atlantic City. Marshall, Joey, unknown fan, Johnny Grande

having to haul our own instruments. So we would drive our own personal cars with our families to most all of the gigs. We wanted to take our families with us because we were gone a lot and we didn't want to miss our families and growing up with our kids. Dick Richards took his wife and babies and Joey took his wife — he didn't have any children during most of the time we were with The Comets and I think just in the last years of The Comets Joey had a daughter. Billy Williamson had children that he took with him and we'd stay in places where the wives could be together and the kids could be together. We'd go visit all the tourist spots, all the places out over Highway 66.

We traveled cross-country by car with our families and tried to look at as many of the tourist places as we could see. We drove on old Highway 66, going out through Missouri, Oklahoma, Texas, New Mexico and Arizona. We would stop and take pictures with those big billboard signs that say "You're Now Entering Oklahoma" or "You're Now Entering Texas," because we'd never been to a lot of those places before. Back in the '50s, Route 66 had outhouses that everybody had to use because they were the only facilities around in some of those way-out places. There were

Indian reservations where the men rode in the cab of the truck and the women rode in the back of the truck in the bed during a snowstorm. I thought that was really quite unique. But things have changed.

The El Cortez Hotel on Fremont Street, Las Vegas

As I mentioned earlier, one of the places we worked was Las Vegas. In 1954, the population of Las Vegas was about 30,000. Now it's 1.5 million! We played at The El Cortez Hotel and Casino, which is still around today. It was on Fremont Street, just a little bit south of the downtown portion of Las Vegas. That was our first encounter with gambling and the state of Nevada, which in those days had no speed limits on its roads.

We went up to Reno, Nevada and played a place there called The Golden Hotel which is no longer in existence. There's a Harrah's there now. But The Golden Hotel was quite a new casino and Harolds Club, one of the older established casinos in Reno, Nevada was right behind it. The Jodimars played Harolds Club in 1957, but I'll go into that later.

Bill Haley and The Comets
at the El Cortez Hotel
Las Vegas, 1954

We did a lot of tourist things — trips up to Virginia City, Nevada and trips to Lake Tahoe in the wintertime, going up over small mountain roads, and visits to the great ski resorts of the Sierras. The highways are six lanes now, but in those days, the roads on the high mountains were pretty narrow.

One cute little thing that happened was with Jim Ferguson. Jim Ferguson used to always wear a hat. We used to pull little pranks on him. Once, in the middle of the summertime we got some limburger cheese and we put it in his hat band. He was walking around with the limburger cheese and the smell was just terrible! He couldn't figure out where the heck the smell was coming from, and so finally we had to own up, that we had pulled a little prank on him.

Another little memorable story happened when we were playing in Kansas City, Missouri. All the Comets were put up in a dormitory-type room where we all had these fold-up beds. One night after our show, I came back and got undressed and lay down across the bed, and the other guys, Billy Williamson, Johnny Grande and Dick and Joey all grabbed the bed and quickly closed it up with me inside of it, like a sandwich.

And they took their belts and they tied the top of it and they rolled me down to the elevator and pushed the elevator button and when the door opened they pushed me in the elevator and ran back to the room. I went down to the little lobby and the door opened and there was a bunch of people waiting to get on the elevator. I was there without my clothes on, sandwiched in this little bed, and I said, "Can somebody get the bell boy and tell him to push me back up to my room, please!" It was funny as hell.

Also, that is the same hotel where Elvis stayed, and I remember the crowd gathering outside the hotel because they knew Elvis was staying there and he opened the window and stuck his leg out and shook it at them. These are the kind of things entertainers did to entertain themselves.

I wish I had an itinerary of all the places that we have played across the United States. One city we played quite often was Cleveland, where Alan "Rock 'n' Roll Everybody" Freed was. There was another Cleveland disc jockey who took a liking to us. His name was Bill Randall. He was responsible for discovering many, many acts and in fact was responsible for introducing Elvis Presley to national TV.

A lot of people think Ed Sullivan gave Elvis his first national TV appearance, but that's not true. The first show that he was on was the *Dorsey Brothers Show*. Bill Randall introduced him. Elvis did our song "Shake, Rattle and Roll" on that show.

Bill was quite a promoter in Cleveland and brought us in for several shows. One I remember very well was at the State Theater. The headliners were Billy Ward and The Dominoes, Bill Haley and The Comets, and a little-known 19-year-old singer by the name of Eydie Gorme. She was just a solo singer at that time, and then of course she met up with her husband Steve Lawrence and they went on to become one of the great nightclub couples of all time. Even at 19, she was really a wonderful singer.

Another notable Cleveland event took place in the auditorium of Brooklyn High School. At the time, Bill Randall was making a documentary on how a disc jockey discovers show business stars. It was called "The Pied Piper of Cleveland" and headlined Bill Haley and The Comets, Pat Boone, The Four Lads, and a young gentleman not too many people had heard of at that time. His name was Elvis Presley.

> The first show that he (Elvis) was
> on was the Dorsey Brothers Show.
> Elvis did our song
> "Shake, Rattle and Roll" on that show.

The film was made and shown one time at the high school auditorium where it was filmed. It was never released as a movie and it disappeared. Up until Bill Randall passed away about a year or two ago, he kept saying he didn't know what had happened to "The Pied Piper of Cleveland" but I believe he sold the film to some out-of-the-country conglomerate or something, and there are other rumors around show business about what happened to the film.

One such rumor is that Colonel Tom Parker bought the film and destroyed it. Nobody knows for sure, but it makes sense that it could have happened because Elvis wasn't the headliner. Maybe some day the film might surface from the people who bought it.

About two, two and a half years ago we came back to do a show at that same auditorium at Brooklyn High School. We performed with The Four Lads. Pat Boone was originally supposed to be there but couldn't make it.

They invited all the students who had been in the audience the night the film was made all those years ago, and a lot of them came. And you know what? They got old! Of course, it was the 50th anniversary of the filming of "Pied Piper." Those kids are all senior citizens now. It was great to meet some of them and talk with them. I really enjoyed being with them. The Four Lads did a great job and we did our show and just knocked them out. They couldn't get over it — we were still in existence and still rockin' around the clock.

Now we move forward to the year 1955 when we were playing in Chicago at the Chicago Theater. "Rock Around the Clock" had become the number one song in the nation, and the popularity of Bill Haley and The Comets was at its height.

We were the headliners of the biggest showcase theater in America. That's where all the stars played. Joe and Dick and I were starting to become very unhappy because we wanted more money. We were working for $175 a week, but we had families to raise, and our regular living expenses. The band paid some of the expenses but not very many.

At the Chicago Theater we asked Bill for a raise. We only wanted $50 a week more, which we felt was not an unreasonable request. We were turned down with the explanation, "We can't afford any more."

Then Dick actually saw a $34,000 royalty check from Decca just lying on the table. After we were refused that raise, we started wondering what kind of a future we were going to have with this band.

We also found out, a day or two later, that all the partners in Bill Haley's band — Bill, Johnny Grande, Billy Williamson and Jim Ferguson — had gone out to a Cadillac agency in Chicago, and each one had bought a brand new Cadillac — and paid cash!

That was the straw that broke the camel's back, because we had asked for a modest raise and were refused, and they were spending outrageous amounts of money on Cadillacs.

That song was
playing simultaneously on
five different radio stations!
I could see "Rock Around the Clock"
was one of the
biggest hits in the country.

We became very close with one of the co-stars of that show at the Chicago Theater, a vocalist by the name of Peggy King. She was featured on the old George Gobel television show, and we used to go to coffee with Peggy and her piano player Eddie Samuels. We'd cry on their shoulders about what was going on.

Peggy said, "Wow, I've seen your show and you guys are a major, major part of it." And she said, "Why don't you start your own band? Why don't you just leave him?" That planted a seed in our minds.

Joe and Dick and I talked about it and we figured, wow, they're never gonna share the rewards of this band with us. We were a talented bunch of young fellows who had ambition and we were definitely not being recognized. So at that point we started making plans to leave Bill Haley's Comets and start our own band.

After the Chicago Theater date we had a few TV appearances and things. We were asked to help drive the new Cadillacs back to Pennsylvania. "Well, yeah," we said, "Brand new Cadillacs, man!" And we drove them.

The one Dick and I rode in had a new kind of a radio with a selectric dial — when you pushed the bar on the radio, it would automatically leave one station and go to another. We were on the New York State Thruway, on our way to Boston first to do a TV show. At about 10 AM, I turned the radio on and "Rock Around the Clock" was playing. I said, "Wow, listen to that. That's us!"

I pushed the bar again while the record played and said, "Let me see if it's playing anywhere else." The dial moved to the next radio station and sure enough, "Rock Around the Clock" was playing there, too. I thought maybe the dial hadn't actually moved, but it had. And I said, "Wow, it's on another station, too!"

Then I pushed a third time and it was playing on a third station, and then I pushed a fourth time and a fifth time. That song was playing simultaneously on five different radio stations!

I could see "Rock Around the Clock" was one of the biggest hits in the country. During the next five minutes I heard it another seven or eight times. "Rock Around the Clock" was on over a dozen times within about a five-minute period.

I knew we had a big hit. I also knew that we were gonna leave Bill Haley's Comets because we were not having any share in any of that success other than providing the music and the show.

We got to Boston for a television show, where we were on the bill with Frankie Lane. He had several big hits at that time but we were the stars of that show because of "Rock Around the Clock."

They had a limousine drive us from the hotel to the theater, and when we got into that limousine the kids mobbed around and were rocking it and shaking it. They wanted to touch us and get a souvenir of anything — a handkerchief, cigarette butt or whatever — anything they could take home with them.

And then we went on home back to Pennsylvania. We had a few days off, so Joe, Dick and I got our band together with some talented local musicians. We recorded a demonstration record. Dick sang, "Rock A Beatin' Boogie" and I sang, "Flip Flop and Fly" on the other side.

We had the Bill Haley sound, because we were the musicians who created it. We just didn't have Bill Haley's voice.

On Labor Day 1955, we gave Bill three weeks' notice. We were playing in Wildwood, New Jersey at a place called Hunt's Pier. Bill offered us a raise at that point to stay but we had already signed a contract with Capitol Records.

During those three weeks they hired four replacement musicians to replace the three of us who went with us to the shows and were instructed to copy the stage performances and antics that we did.

The last show we did with Bill was at a magnificent ballroom at the Broadwood

Hotel in Philadelphia. About a week or so later, Joey, Dick and I drove to New York for our first recording session at Capitol Records.

We got our band together and
someone introduced us to Larry Taylor,
a band manager and promoter.
We gave him a copy of our
demonstration record and he took it
to Capitol Records in New York.
He got us a $5,000 advance and a great
record contract with Capitol Records.

The Jodimars

We started thinking about what to call our band. We were going to call ourselves The Juniors because of Bill Haley calling us junior partners. Then we started toying around with syllables of our first names — Joe, Dick and Marshall. Jo-Di-Mars! It was originally the Mardijoes and the Dimarjoes but neither of those sounded as good as the Jodimars. So Jodimars it was.

We got our band together and someone introduced us to Larry Taylor, a band manager and promoter. We gave him a copy of our demonstration record and he took it to Capitol Records in New York. He got us a $5,000 advance and a great record contract with Capitol Records.

We hired Frank Pingatore, who had worked for Bill Haley and The Comets and written "Two Hound Dogs," "Happy Baby" and several other songs. Frank was unhappy because Bill wasn't recording as much material as he wanted recorded. He saw we were a band that had a great chance to make it and started writing songs for us. I was into songwriting in those days and he and I co-wrote quite a few songs together.

One of the songs Frank and I wrote together was one of our first Capitol Records releases, "Let's All Rock Together."

The Jodimars: Charlie Hess, Dick Richards, Marshall, Max Daffner, Joey Ambrose

Frank wrote the flip side song, which turned out to be one of the most popular in our recording career. It was sung by Dick Richards and was called "Well Now Dig This." For the introduction to that song, they brought in a boatsman from the Brooklyn Navy Yard to blow a boatsman's whistle because they wanted it to sound authentic. The song started out with a whistle blow and I said, "Well, now dig this" (like "Now hear this" on the ships.)

That song made quite a bit of noise in the recording field but it wasn't a hit — at least in America. But we found out it was a hit in a lot of other places like England and Australia.

It sold well enough to pay back Capitol Records' advance and some royalty checks for us. "Well Now Dig This" was Capitol's sixth best seller in November 1955, but behind five other major hits.

In fact, it became so popular in England that years later they named a magazine after the song. The magazine was actually called

Well Now Dig This. They even used a clip from the song on their answering machine. That lasted for years, and for all I know it's still there.

> "Clarabella" didn't do much
> for us when we recorded it,
> but there was a young
> upstart group from England
> by the name of The Beatles
> that liked the song.
> They recorded it and put it on
> the "Live at the BBC" album.

The magazine is still in business and is one of the most highly respected magazines for rock 'n' roll enthusiasts in the world. They've been in business for well over 20 years and have done quite a few good spreads about The Jodimars. Bill Haley is also one of the big guns that they promote, of course.

Frank Pingatore and I wrote a couple of other songs. One was "Eat Your Heart Out Annie." Another was "Clarabella," named after my sister Clara Belle.

"Clarabella" didn't do much for us when we recorded it, but there was a young upstart group from England by the name of The Beatles that liked the song. They recorded it and put it on the "Live at the BBC" album. "Clarabella" is sung by Paul McCartney.

That song went on and sold millions of copies, but my income from it has been next to nothing. Frank promised me co-writer's royalties but I never got them. I guess if you don't have it in writing, you don't have it. I learned from those experiences. But more importantly, I know what the truth is. And when you know what the truth is, you can sleep at night.

When Capitol Records brought us in for our first recording session, we rehearsed the songs before going to the studio. We had a wonderful guitar player named Charlie Hess who played on all the Jodimar records. But they wanted to have a little larger sound, so on the first session they added Tony Mattola who played the lead guitar solo along with Charlie, and it's a really great guitar solo.

Our closing number, "Straight Jacket,"
with me doing the stagecraft
and antics with the bass and
pulling Joey around on the bass
caused such a frenzy that we were
actually asked to tone down our act.

Tony Mattola, who was quite famous, also jobbed out to play recording sessions. The second recording session we did they hired another great guitar player by the name of George Barnes. George Barnes is a world-famous jazz guitarist who ended up playing on several of our recordings.

Our first show as the Jodimars was at the Palace Theater in New York. We even had Judy Garland's old dressing room, with her name still on the door. After that, we began an extensive tour of the Eastern United States and Canada. We played the major rock 'n' roll venues, including the Alan Freed 'Easter Jubilee of Stars' at the Brooklyn Paramount Theater in April 1956. The bill included The Platters and Frankie Lymon and The Teenagers among many other of

The Jodimars at the Palace Theater, 1955

the big rock 'n' roll acts of the day. Our closing number, "Straight Jacket," with me doing the stagecraft and antics with the bass and pulling Joey around on the bass caused such a frenzy that we were actually asked to tone down our act. The New York Police were concerned about reports of rioting at similar shows and wanted to keep control of the audience by patrolling the aisles. *Billboard* magazine referred to the police presence at the show as creating an Alcatraz-like atmosphere in the audience, compared to the riotous goings-on on stage.

The Jodimars at The Riptide Club, Wildwood NJ, summer 1956 at an afternoon matinee.
L-R: Joey Ambrose, Marshall Lytle, Max Daffner, Chuck Hess, Dick Richards

Sometimes they overbooked the theaters and kids wanted to dance. The kids would be dancing in the aisles and the police would try to squelch the dancing and make them sit down and they didn't want to sit down. They wanted to stand up and have a good time. The police apparently didn't want them to have a good time. So they started pushing the kids around and the kids got angry and fought back and busted up chairs and got up on the stage and it was quite a situation that had occurred.

Our success at that show earned us a spot on Alan Freed's TV show in May, 1956 and on the national Kate Smith TV Show.

Our recording career with the Jodimars was out in left field, and I say that with my heart in my hand because the heartbeat of Capitol Records was in Hollywood, California. And we were recording in New York City.

When the first Jodimars' record was

released in late 1955, Capitol Records was riding on such a high. Frank Sinatra had a big hit. Nelson Riddle had a big hit with "Lisbon Antigua" and Nat King Cole had a hit. Tennessee Ernie Ford had "Sixteen Tons" and Kay Starr also had a big hit at that time. Just about every other Hollywood artist on Capitol Records had a hit record, so they didn't promote guys who were recording in New York City as much as they could have.

Had we recorded in Hollywood, Capitol would have gotten behind us a whole lot more. Our records were just kind of released and if something happened, something happened. But we ourselves didn't follow up on our recording careers the way we should have.

We wanted to have a nightclub act so we created a good one and took it to Reno, Nevada in 1957. We found ourselves working in Nevada for many years because that's where the big nightclub money was. We were working at Harolds Club, which you may

The Jodimars at Harolds Club, Reno Nevada, 1957

remember from earlier in this book. That was the top place in Reno at that time. Harolds had literally hundreds of billboards all across America that said "Harolds Club or Bust." It was reported that they even had one up in Alaska or some place that said "Harolds Club — 2,000 some odd miles away."

We went on to become a big hit in Reno. Our first show was supposed to be for four weeks and lasted about 20. Then we were signed for three additional years with options and, boy, we were flying high.

Our recording career just sat there and didn't do much, so we concentrated on the nightclub portion because we were making pretty good money. Later on in 1957 we went on tour with Tony Martin and Tex Benecke's orchestra. It was 30 days of one-nighters and traveling in a bus, and very interesting.

In 1958, wanting to improve on what we already had, we became friends with Louie Prima's orchestra, which played Harrah's.

The Jodimars, 1958

Harrah's was right next door, so after our shows we used to go over and watch Louie Prima in the lounge. We became good friends with his drummer, Bobby Morris, and his trombone player, James "Little Red" Blount. Those two were unhappy with Louie and were looking for some way to expand.

Joe and Dick and I, who were the leaders of the band, starting talking about bringing Bobby with us as our drummer, and letting Max Dafner go. We hired him and Little Red. Unfortunately, Little Red lasted with us only two or three weeks. Vince James, who was our guitar player and comedian at that time, wanted to retire and head back to Pennsylvania, so we let him go too, and hired a comedian named Al Antonio. Al was married to a lady named Audrey, and she was a beautiful, beautiful girl. She was a dancer, and we created quite an act. We bought some gorilla suits and had a jungle show with the gorillas in this box, and it was a great sight.

Since our recording career had fallen away to nothing, we left Harolds Club in 1958 and came back to New York to record a couple of songs. One was called "Shoe Sue," on which I did the vocal, and the other was called "Story Tellin' Baby," written by Damita Joe who at that time was married to Steve Gibson of The Red Caps.

One morning after our show,
I was walking through the coffee shop
and Mr. (Gary) Cooper stopped me
on my way past his table and said,
"Hey, young man, have breakfast with me."
What a thrill that was.

We thought, wow, man, we got some great sounds on this thing. Everybody liked the songs, but they were on a small label. They had no distribution and it was not one of the high-powered majors. The songs didn't do anything, so we spruced up the Jodimars group and we started traveling again.

We took our show back to Reno and Harolds Club again. We also played the Dunes Hotel in Las Vegas and a lot of other places there, including the Sands Hotel, opposite the magnificent Ella Fitzgerald.

Ella was every performer's favorite singer. She would go on about 10 or 11 at night. She'd play for an hour, and then we would come on and we'd play for an hour. We had the shift, I think, from 12 midnight to 6 AM. When we would go on, the whole audience would be full of stars who had all come to hear Ella Fitzgerald sing. When she left the stage, they stayed and we entertained them. It was one of the highlights of 1958 and our careers.

Gary Cooper used to catch our last show in the morning before he would go to breakfast. He was filming a movie just on the outskirts of Vegas. He would stand in the back of the room and watch our show. One morning after our show, I was walking through the coffee shop and Mr. Cooper stopped me on my way past his table and said, "Hey, young man, have breakfast with me." What a thrill that was. He was a wonderful guy and just like he was in the movies.

We got to know a lot of the Vegas entertainers because they all came in and out of the Sands. Later we went back up to Reno again. We would bounce back and forth between Reno, Lake Tahoe and Las Vegas.

In late '58, we were back again in Reno and things were not going well for the Jodimars. So, after one of our engagements, I went to Hollywood to look for a new record contract, and Joe and Dick headed back to Pennsylvania with their families.

I had to seek a new recording contract because our contract with Capitol had expired and they didn't pick up the option on us. We had done twelve sides with Capitol and the sales just didn't happen.

I went to Imperial Records to talk to the owner and producer, Lou Chudd. I told him who I was and what I had. I played him a couple of the Jodimars' records and he liked them. He said "Yeah, let's do some sides with you guys" and we signed a contract.

I called Joe and Dick and told them about it, and they said, "Oh, we're on our way back to Philadelphia, so why don't you just go ahead and do the session by yourself."

Imperial Records had a house band that they used on all of Ricky Nelson's records. Imperial gave me four songs to do with them, but the record label would still say it was the Jodimars.

I recorded the songs and nothing happened. I kept wondering, when are they going to release them? Imperial Records just never did release them. I heard rumors that Ozzie Nelson wouldn't let them be released because I had used Ricky's band. I kind of understood why Ozzie would have been upset, so it didn't bother me.

Joe and Dick were just no longer interested in the Jodimars, so we split up in early 1959 and I went on to create another group.

Elvis was giving all the
entertainers backstage
a demonstration on karate,
because he held a black belt.

He was actually showing us
how to pull a guy's eyeball out.

Tommy Page and The Page Boys

In 1959, I created a lounge group with Jimmy Bryant, one of the very best guitar players in the world. We played around Nevada, because that's where the money was. We played in Winnemucca and Elko. We hired Jimmy's old partner, Speedy West, who was available at that time.

While playing in Winnamucka, we ran across a friend of Jimmy's, an old B cowboy movie star named Lash LaRue. Lash had been one of my heroes when I was a little boy going to theaters back in the forties, the era of Roy Rogers and Gene Autry. Lash was working at a brewery in downtown Los Angeles and was just chomping at the bit to get back into show business. We hired him.

Lash had an act where he could cut a cigarette right out of somebody's mouth with a black snake whip. I trusted him enough to let him cut a cigarette out of my mouth on our show!

We took him to Winnemucca with us for a week. There wasn't much money for a little show like that — probably just a couple hundred apiece — so we just shared what we made. We did that one week in Winnemucca and boy, I'll tell you, that was so exciting for me. It was quite a memory for me with my childhood hero, Lash LaRue.

That group didn't last very long, and I met another young singer and guitar player named Wes Buchanan in late '59. We created a little group with a drummer and an accordion and headed off to play in Fairbanks, Alaska.

I think we went there in the summertime. Our nightclub was located just on the outskirts of town. We had some pretty decent crowds but it was a challenge keeping that up after one of the competitors down the street brought in a bunch of dancers from the states.

I say "from the states" because in 1959 Alaska had just become a state and was still acting like it was a territory. There were some pretty dangerous guys up there. The fellow who owned the nightclub was a member of the Purple gang out of Detroit. He liked us a lot.

One night after our show, I noticed that one of our stage lights had burned out. It was a large bulb. I unscrewed it and took it to the owner and I said "Is there any way I could get another one of these to light up the stage?" He said, "Oh, yeah, I got a great use for that." And he took the burned-out bulb.

I heard later that he had taken the insides out of the bulb, filled it with gasoline, put a wick in it and threw it in the window of our competitor down the street, burning his nightclub to the ground. The fire department came to the scene and stood there and watched it burn because the nightclub was just past the city limits and out of the fire department's jurisdiction. But we didn't have any competition after that! It was just one of the crazy things that happened in my life.

In early 1960, Wes and I were playing in Las Vegas, jumping around different places and visiting entertainers. We liked to do that.

We went backstage one night in 1960 at the Sahara Hotel to say hello to people we knew. Elvis Presley was there with his entourage. He had just gotten out of the Army, and he was backstage saying hello to people just like we were. Elvis was giving all the entertainers backstage a demonstration on karate, because he held a black belt.

He was actually showing us how to pull a guy's eyeball out. You aim your finger at his ear with your thumb sticking out in a karate stance, and then, if you just push your finger towards the guy's ear, your thumb goes in his eyeball, and then you just pull it out. It's kind of gross!

During this demonstration, Elvis handed his wristwatch to me and asked me to hold it. The back of the watch said,

To Elvis Presley
Congratulations on the sale
of your 79,000,000 record.
From RCA Victor

Wow! He had been a star for only four years and he had sold 79 million records. What a star he was. And yet he was just a regular guy, gathered together with the rest of us, telling stories and stuff.

Wes Buchanan and I stayed together for about a year or so and recorded a couple of songs. One of them was "One Grain of Sand." It didn't do much, and neither did the other, the title of which I've forgotten. Meanwhile, I was on my own again, trying as always to make some money in show business.

I went to my agent in Beverly Hills, California. He told me the name "Marshall Lytle" was worn out. He said, "Let's try a different name. Why don't we call you Tommy Page. What do you think of that name? Tommy Page. And we'll call your band 'The Page Boys — Tommy Page and The Page Boys.'"

So we worked up some new publicity and booked us out as Tommy Page and The Page Boys. In fact that was also right at the time just before Wes was leaving and so I think Wes and I played Las Vegas together.

We were looking for all kinds of possibilities and so we just kind of jobbed around and then I had a chance to go back to Alaska again and Wes had already moved on. So I created another group and took it to Alaska.

We had a very good guitar player and

singer named Chuck Steele. We hired an accordion player and a drummer who went with us, and we went back to Fairbanks, Alaska and played that same place Wes and I had played before.

We did really well there, only this time it was in the winter...and cold! Alaska is "The Land of the Midnight Sun," but that's just in summer. In winter, the sun never came up and it was dark and cold all the time.

We spent a lot of time indoors. There was a little lady down the street from where we were staying, who sang in a small hotel nightclub with a piano player. Her name was Sonja Lee, and we got acquainted very quickly. In fact, after a couple of weeks we decided we wanted to get married.

She called home and told her mom and dad she wanted to get married. She was only 19 years old at that time. She was still a virgin and would remain a virgin until after we got married.

Her parents said "Do us a favor. Come

back here to Oakland and do it right; get married back here." That was fine with me. But Sonja's contract ended about three or four weeks before mine, so she flew back home to Oakland and I stayed in Fairbanks until just before Christmas. We communicated by letter every day. Everything was just fine, and then I finally flew down there and got to meet all of her friends and parents.

They had a wedding shower and her girlfriends all came. I was put on display and it was a fun time for me. I stayed at her parents' home for the few months prior to our wedding. Sonja and I got married in Reno, Nevada on April 2, 1961.

During the months prior to the wedding, I re-created Tommy Page and the Page Boys with Sonja Lee as our vocalist.

There were a couple of different bands that played with us and we went on the road together. We played some nightclubs in Albuquerque, New Mexico, and traveled and played all over the western United States.

It was difficult to save any money when we had to eat out all the time and stay in hotels, so we bought a 28-foot travel trailer. We had a '59 Cadillac at that time, and we rigged it up with the trailer. That was our home and we took it with us. We were finally able to save money and become better organized financially.

Tommy Page and The Pageboys with Sonja Lee

We pulled that house trailer across the Rocky Mountains about five times. We played in Colorado Springs, Colorado. We played up in South Dakota. We played St. Louis, Missouri and Springfield, Illinois, as well as a lot of small towns across America.

It wasn't difficult to get a booking because our price was not that high. We never did pursue a recording career, but we probably should have because we had a good sound.

We ended up with a cute little show where I did a lot of comedy. We hired a gentleman by the name of Randy Stewart, who was an accordion player and a very fine vocalist with a voice and style very similar to that of Tennessee Ernie Ford.

Randy was a great straight man and he and I created lots of cute comedy skits. Our nightclub show became quite good, and I am happy to say that we kept that group together until I got out of show business in 1967.

We played a lot of places, and Sonja and I never had any children until she decided in 1967 that it was time. Back in the early part of our marriage she had said, "What are we going to call our children? You're known as Tommy Page now, so let's make it legal. What do you think?" So we went to a courthouse in Oakland, California and I changed my legal name from Marshall Lytle to Tommy Page. And I am still, to this day, legally, Tommy Page.

Our children starting arriving. Jeffrey Page was born on my birthday in 1967 — quite a birthday present. Then came Adam Page. Then Jason Page. And finally, came the twins, Melissa and Ryan Page, who were born in 1975.

I became a real estate agent in the state of California in 1967 and was introduced to land sales, which were very, very big at that time. They were being pitched as an investment — half acre, one acre, two acre and three acre parcels in the foothills near the San Joaquin Valley, where the gold was discovered.

It all started when I went to a meeting led by Jeff Dennis, who had one of the greatest sales forces I had ever seen. He was a true motivator of men. I said, "My god, these guys are making thousands and thousands of dollars every week. If I could do just half that good it would be great."

So I went and got my real estate license and I became a very good salesman. And I made a good living. I was climbing the ladder of success, so to speak. First I was a salesman, and then I became a manager, and then they offered me a position to run a division, and then I was offered a position to run an entire project. I was in charge of my own sales force selling over $200 million of real estate.

By the mid-seventies, however, the attractiveness of land sales had dwindled due to bad publicity ("It's not a good investment") and I started looking for another avenue to pursue.

When the bottom fell out of the land sales business, I became a real estate agent and started selling houses instead of land. That went pretty well for me too.

Then I got my real estate broker's license, and then I wanted to run my own company, so I became part owner of one with two other brokers. We owned three real estate offices in California — one in Pleasanton, one in Dublin, and one in Livermore.

Although I was doing quite well in real estate, Sonja Lee decided she didn't want to be married to me anymore. I guess I was spending more time at my work than I was at marriage. At least that's what I was told. When she told me she wanted a divorce, I didn't fight it.

She had hired a lawyer, so I hired one too to try and protect myself — which I wasn't able to do very well because, in California, the woman gets the oil well and the man gets the shaft. That's what happened to me. I had once been a member of the Saddlemen, and now I was saddled with over $1,800 a month in child support.

About a month after the divorce was final, Sonja said she was going to sell the house and move to Oregon. She remarried and took our children up to Oregon, and apparently they lived happily ever after.

I never realized it but it was very difficult for me to see my children, being way up there in Oregon and having a real estate schedule and trying to maintain that family. So anyway my life changed quite a bit, and so did hers.

The last time I saw Bill Haley I believe was in 1974 or '75 in Hayward, California. He was playing in a little nightclub and I had gone  to see him. He was very cordial, and he introduced me to his audience as his original bass player. Later, he invited me back to his dressing room and he introduced me to his new Mexican wife, Martha. And he said, "We just had a new baby!" And I said, "Oh, what did you name it?" And he said, "Pedro." I had a hard time keeping a straight face because Pedro Haley just didn't sound like those two names belonged together.

Bill Haley
1925-1981

I invited him to come to my home for dinner and he said he'd like to but he had some plans with his wife. Then he said, "I'm doing a little drinking right now. I've been drinking about a fifth of tequila every day." I never knew Bill as an alcoholic or a drinker but I guess he had turned into one. That was my last encounter with Bill on a physical basis.

Then in 1981 when the news came out that he had passed, somehow the news media in San Francisco got hold of it and called me. I was a real estate broker in Livermore, California at that particular time. They brought the news cameras over and they conducted an interview with me. They were going to put it on the national news, but that day when it came time to go on the air they had another big story about a fire in Las Vegas — the hotel fire that consumed so many lives. So they pre-empted my interview about Bill Haley and instead put the story about the fire on the national news.

I went on in the real estate business, selling homes in Livermore. I got interested in a lady who was one of my agents. Her name was Jeanne McGee.

Jeanne and I created a romance and started seeing each other, and finally I said, "Let's combine our families...you know."

She had a young son and several other children by another marriage. I tried this a few times and then I quit asking her.

But then, finally, one day she said, "Well what about that, combining our families' routine? Let's do it." So we got married in 1978, and Jeanne McGee became Jeanne Page. We each sold our houses and bought another house in a nice neighborhood. It was a nice large home with a swimming pool, and things were rolling along.

I sold a home to a fellow named Bill Farrell, who was a United Airlines pilot. We became good friends and one day he said, "You ever think about learning how to fly?" I said, "I've always wanted to learn."

He said, "Well, I'm an instructor and if you'd like to learn how to fly I'll teach you for free." I jumped at that chance. He said, "You just rent the airplane and I'll teach you how to fly it."

I went home and told Jeanne that Bill wanted to teach me how to fly. She said, "I want to learn, too." So he agreed to teach both of us how to fly.

We started renting airplanes in the Livermore area. We'd fly up to Reno and have lunch, or we'd go down to Monterey and have lunch, or we'd go down to Las Vegas and have lunch. We even planned a weekend down in Las Vegas and took Joey Ambrose, the saxophonist from The Comets, and his son for an airplane ride out over Lake Mead and Hoover Dam. It was an exciting time.

After Jeanne and I became licensed, we used to fly ourselves. Once we rented an airplane and flew down to visit some friends in San Diego. It was a Cessna 182RG with a retractable gear. We flew it from Livermore right down to San Diego. Our trip took us right across the Los Angeles International Airport's air corridor.

Everything went great on the way down. But on the way back, when we were flying right across the Los Angeles airport, I looked across the instrument panel and all the lights went out! All my electrical power had just gone away. I had lost all radio contact and I said, "Uh oh, we're in trouble." But the fan to the engine was still running like a dream. So I said to Jeanne, "Let's see if we can find a place to set this thing down."

We were headed north, right out over Beverly Hills and finally Jeanne saw several possible landing places. One was the Van Nuys airport, but I said, "No, I don't want to land at Van Nuys, it's too busy an airport. Find me one that's not as busy."

Off to the west near the coast was the Camarillo airport, near Oxnard. We flew over there and on the way I had to put the gear down manually because it was a retractable gear and the gear was electric. It had a pumping mechanism where you could pump this handle and the landing gear would come down out of the fuselage, and it would be visible, so that you could see that it was down. But having no electrical power, I could not confirm that the landing gear was in a locked position.

We arrived at the Camarillo Airport and I did one fly by the tower and waved my wings at them for a signal to land, and I didn't get one. So I said, "I'm gonna put this thing down anyway." And fortunately, I did.

We taxied up to a Cessna dealer that was about to close for the day because it was about six o' clock. They sent me to a mechanic working out of one of his hangars. We taxied on down to where he was located, and he told us we would have to leave the plane there overnight.

After we got settled in I called the flying school that had rented us the airplane. I talked to the head guy and told him about the electrical problem. He said, "Oh, did that airplane do that again?" I said "What do you mean, again?"

And he said, "Well, if you just turn the master switch off and turn it back on again, the problem will cure itself." And I said "You son of a bitch, there's nothing mentioned in these log books about that. You could have killed us!" I was furious at this point and I said, "You're paying for our hotel room and you're paying for our expenses while we're here." He agreed to do that.

We stayed overnight and the next morning the service man at the hangar said, "It was just a dead battery. I charged the battery and now it starts and stops like a champ."

We got in the plane and flew it all the way back to Livermore, which was several hours' flying time, right out over the mountains. We landed and I returned the airplane to the rental guy. I immediately said to Jeanne, "We're going to have to find our own airplane so we don't have to worry about these kinds of problems again."

I asked a couple of people there at the airport and one them said "There's a fellow down here who's got a Beechcraft Bonanza he wants to sell. I got a hold of him and looked at it, and it was a nice old airplane. It was a 1949 A model with a B tail, retractable gear, and a good engine. It ran like a champ but needed some upgrading on the radio equipment. So I made a deal with him to buy the airplane and get his hangar, since hangars were hard to get.

Jeanne and I just loved that airplane and we flew a lot of different places. We'd fly up to Reno for a weekend, or we'd fly down to Santa Monica or Half Moon Bay, or just take a ride out over the San Francisco Bay and fly over the Golden Gate Bridge for sightseeing. When you own your own airplane, you get to create your own schedule and travel itinerary. It was a joy.

In 1981, Jeanne and I took the vacation of a lifetime. We took 22 days off from the real estate business and went flying. We

Marshall's Beechcraft Bonanza, Livermore, California

wanted to visit friends and family. We took our V tail Beechcraft Bonanza. We flew a circle around the United States taking the southern route and visiting my brother

Johnny and his wife Freddie in Bullhead City, Arizona, and my brother Clifford and his family in Phoenix.

Marshall flying his Beechcraft Bonanza back to Livermore, California from Lake Tahoe, 1981

Going east then up the east coast we had a brief visit with my brother Gene and my children Marshall and Larry. I had my son Rodney with me in my airplane. We had picked him up in Norfolk, Virginia where he was stationed in the Navy. We then flew into Reading, Pennsylvania where my son Marshall lived with his family and I was able to give Marshall and my Grandson Matt Lytle their first airplane ride. It was a great visit. We even flew into Montreal, Canada, and returned flying over the northern states back to our home in Livermore, California. We flew over 7,000 miles and it was a great trip. We flew halfway across the United States in a little single engine airplane! That was something that we would never forget as long as we were on this earth.

After that, the real estate market started to turn a little sour, and we had an opportunity to sell our Beechcraft Bonanza, the A model, to a friend of ours in Southern California. We took the money and bought a 1951 Beechcraft Bonanza, C model.

We were having financial difficulties with our real estate office, because interest rates had jumped up to 21% in 1981. Virtually nobody was buying real estate. We had to sell some properties just to survive. We finally sold our real estate offices to one of our dear buddies. We sold our home, getting out from under that big mortgage, and then we went down to San Diego and rented a little house.

I was looking for something to do. We got involved in a couple of ventures that didn't work out, and then I met a young man by the name of Al Robinson, a great guy who was with the Albert J. Lowry real estate school. They gave seminars on how to buy houses with little or no money down. I became a traveling speaker and was very successful at it. We would sell a weekend seminar for $495 in different cities throughout the United States and Canada.

I made very good money doing this. We moved from San Diego up to West Lake Village, California, a very upscale neighborhood north of Los Angeles and the headquarters of Al Lowry's company. Jeanne and I became close friends with Al Lowry and his wife, and even bought a big Fleetwood Brougham Cadillac from them that was practically brand new.

For a while, things went very well indeed. We even bought a boat. But then the seminar business began to falter.

We went into the rehearsal hall
and naturally I still knew
"Rock Around the Clock"
from having played it so many times.

After about an hour of rehearsals,
it all started to come back to us.
We started sounding just like
we did in the fifties.

And the Band Played On

As luck would have it, in 1987, I got a phone call from Dick Richards, who said there was an opportunity to have a reunion with all of the original Comets. I thought that was really great because it did not interfere with any other ideas — it was only one show. Dick had his producer provide us all with airfare, a hotel, instruments and a rehearsal room.

Remember, the original Comets had not seen each other or played together for over 25 years. Two of the guys, Franny Beecher and Johnny Grande, we hadn't seen for

The Comets reunion show,
Philadelphia, 1987

32 years. When we got to Philadelphia, we entered the hotel lobby and walked right past them without even recognizing them. In 32 years, people can change, and they did — they got old. And I imagine we did too!

We went into rehearsal. Now keep in mind that we had all gotten out of the music business. Dick had acted in Broadway plays and movies, and Joey still played saxophone on weekends sometimes, but he was a pit boss at Caesar's Palace in Las Vegas. I had been a public speaker in the real estate business. For the past 20 years, I had never even thought of performing again.

We went into the rehearsal hall and naturally I still knew "Rock Around the Clock" from having played it so many times. We started performing "Shake, Rattle and Roll" and "Rock Around the Clock" because those were Bill Haley's two biggest hits. After about an hour of rehearsals, it all started to come back to us. We started sounding just like we did in the fifties.

It was like riding a bicycle. Once you know how to ride one, I guess you never really forget. But just the same, it was gratifying to hear ourselves start to gel again musically.

In the show we were to do they had us playing behind another artist from Philadelphia, Charlie Gracie. Charlie had a song called "Butterfly" that was a big hit in 1957, going to number one. Charlie was going to do "Butterfly" and we would back him up. We rehearsed "Butterfly" with Charlie and it was exciting, and he did a

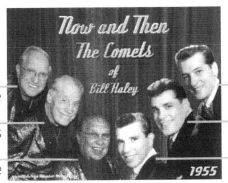

Marshall Lytle

Dick Richards

Joey Ambrose

great job with it. Then they had some other kid on the show who wanted to sing a blues song, and we backed him up too.

But the main thing was that we did two songs, "Shake, Rattle and Roll" and "Rock Around the Clock."

We had a full house at the Academy of Music. The Academy was built around 1858 and is quite possibly the most historic music venue in the United States after Carnegie Hall. (In the 1950s, we were the first rock act to ever play at Carnegie Hall.) A countless number of world-famous musical artists had played there.

The Academy of Music was putting on a show honoring Dick Clark for his achievements with American Bandstand, which you may recall was originally broadcast from Philadelphia. They were giving Dick Clark a star on Broad Street, kind of like the ones on Hollywood Boulevard. They had done this for others in the Philadelphia area who had achieved greatness in music and the arts. In fact, this section of Broad Street had been renamed "The Avenue of the Arts."

The show featured about 40 different acts that started out in the Philadelphia area. I won't try to name them all, but they included Frankie Avalon, Fabian, Bobby Rydell, Chubby Checker, Patti LaBelle, and, of course, Bill Haley and The Comets had started near Philadelphia in a little town called Chester.

We had been featured on *American Bandstand* way back in 1954 when we first started promoting our record. At the time, the show was being run not by Dick Clark but by its original creator Bob Horn. In the mid-1950s, however, Bob got in trouble with a young teenage girl and WFIL, which produced the show, fired him. They replaced him with Dick Clark, who prior to that had been a TV personality for commercials on WFIL. By 1957, *American Bandstand* was so successful that Dick Clark was able to take it national, where it was broadcast from Hollywood every afternoon. The rest, as they say, is history.

We went on and did our portion of the show at The Academy of Music in Philadelphia that night in 1987. We did very well. We were in fact the only act that *Entertainment Tonight* picked up when they did a brief segment on the success of the show. Right after our performance, people kept coming up to us and telling us how good it was to have us back together again.

An attorney from New York by the name of David Hirschberg came to us and he said, "Boy, you guys really brought back some memories." He had been a Bill Haley fan from way back. He said, "If I could get you guys a gig over in England, would you be willing to do it?" We said, "Oh sure," never thinking anything would ever happen with it.

But about a year later he called us up. He had scheduled us to go to England in November 1989 and do a show featuring The Comets and The Jodimars. Joe, Dick, and I, and Johnny, Billy, and Franny were the original Comets. (Billy Williamson had completely wiped Bill Haley and The Comets from his life after he left the band, and moved back to Pennsylvania.) Joe and Dick and I were the original Jodimars. So he had booked Joe, Dick and me in two acts for that engagement in England. Just the same, we agreed to split the money equally among all five of us.

We were to do a full show with the Jodimars, and then a full show with The Comets. It was wonderful to get back together again, but we really did not think many people were going to show up. It turned out, however, that over 3,000 people had bought tickets and paid over $50 apiece to see and hear us.

When we got to England, we had a list of songs we were going to do, but we did not know the arrangements. We had recorded the songs so many years earlier that we had simply forgotten how we had played them.

So we hired this young group called the Stargazers to back us up and show us how we did our songs. At some of our rehearsals the Stargazers would do our songs and then

The Jodimars at a rehearsal with three of The Stargazers
L-R: Marshall; Joey; Stargazers Piano, Chris Gardner;
Dick; Stargazers Drummer, Ricky Brawn;
and Guitar, Pete Davenport
1989 at Breen Sands in South Wales

say, "That's how you did it." And then we'd
try them and they'd say "No, no you've got
the guitar part wrong or you've got the
saxophone part wrong, or you've got this
wrong." They showed us what we used to
do when we recorded. So there we were,
learning how to do our songs from a group
of youngsters.

There was a young singer in London
who sounded like a British Bill Haley. His
name was Jocko Buddin. All the guys seemed
to think that we ought to hire him. I was not

sure we needed him, but eventually I agreed. We used him for a number of years, to the point where it would have been unthinkable to tour England or Europe without him.

We even had him come to America to sing with us here on numerous occasions, until the authorities at US Customs finally noticed he did not have a green card. He bragged about being a member of The Comets, but they were not impressed. They sent him back to England and we had to perform without him. And we managed to do so very well.

We found that we did not really need Jocko. It was Bill Haley's Comets that people wanted to hear, and they knew Bill Haley was dead — so anybody who sang his songs just put a new voice to the old music, and that was fine. As it happened, I became the vocalist who sang Bill Haley's hits.

But back to that first performance in England. Included in the crowd of 3,000 were several people from continental Europe, including Klaus Kettner, our current promoter and long-time friend, who had traveled all the way from Munich, Germany. Klaus was a just a skinny, dark-haired 25-year-old lad at the time. He expressed interest in bringing us to Germany to do a show, and we agreed.

Our first show with Klaus was in 1991. It was like a New Year's Eve or festival show, and it featured the Stargazers (who had come in from England) and other acts from the area. It snowed really, really hard but we had a packed house and boy, we knocked 'em out. Everybody was having a wonderful time.

At that show we met a wonderful group from England that performed under the name of Bill Haley Revival Band. It was a group of young musicians who copied Bill Haley and The Comets. They asked our permission to do so and we were happy to give it. They became friends of ours. They seemed awed by our presence and wanted to have breakfast with us the next morning.

At breakfast we paired off, with each musician in the Bill Haley Revival Band sitting across from his counterpart in The Comets. The bass player, of course wanted to sit with me. He spoke broken English, and said something to me that was really quite entertaining to me at the time. "Being in your presence gives me chicken skin." I said "Gives you what?" "Chicken skin," he repeated. Suddenly I realized he was trying to say "goose bumps."

This young man went on to do all of my antics with the bass. He played very, very good bass, and his group really paid great tribute to Bill Haley and The Comets. They still do a lot of shows in Europe as a Bill Haley's Comets revival band.

Ricky Brawn of the Stargazers became a real close friend of mine after our first engagement there in 1987, and in about 1990 he came to visit me in Florida. He had the idea that on my next visit to England we could do a country and western album with me doing the singing. So he and I became partners and created this album as Marshall and the Shooting Stars. We put up the money and created a pretty darn good CD out of it, and we sold it to a record company in Tokyo. We got our money back out of it, and even though nothing more happened with the recording, it was something I was proud to have done.

Another thing I did was with a songwriter named Warren Farren. He and I wrote a song together called "The Viagara Rock" and we recorded it with The Comets and started doing it in our show. People really loved it. In Florida, it was the number one requested song at three different radio stations! But unfortunately we were with a small label out of Las Vegas that had no distribution, and they did not do a darn thing with it. We sold a few copies in England and a few places, and that was about it.

We gave Klaus the exclusive right to book us throughout Europe. It got to the point where we would come and do a week in England, and then two weeks in Germany or Austria, and then Klaus would book us in Hungary, Spain, Switzerland and elsewhere.

We have played just about everywhere you can play in Europe, and we still enjoy going to Europe and doing tours for Klaus.

We have a promoter in England by the name of Richie Gee. He owned a place called The Tennessee Club which was a rock 'n' roll venue, and he would also do a show in the ballroom of a local golf course outside of the London area. Then he started doing festivals, which he does to this day.

The most recent one we did for him was called "The Wildest Cats in Town." We did it at Pontins by the Sea in Lowestoft, England. It is right on the seashore of the North Sea. We also headlined there in July 2009.

When we do a show for Richie Gee he usually brings us into town in a very unique way. One year he brought us in on the train and all the people from the local area met us at the train depot. It was like the time Bill Haley did his first tour of England back in 1957 — they arrived on the Queen Mary and then took England by storm.

They still love us in England. We have played just about every city there. We enjoy going back. One year Richie Gee hired a big old helicopter and all five of us were on the helicopter and landed in the middle of a big park right by the downtown area of Lowestoft. He had a parade all set up. You would have thought the Queen of England herself was there. People were standing on the street waving as we went by in a big double decker bus. The mayor of the city was there, along with all the press and cameras. It was really heartwarming to be part of a scene like that.

We know how the Beatles must have felt when they first came to America, because it is like that when we go back to England sometimes. The fans show us tremendous affection.

After playing Europe several times a year for many years, plus many gigs around the United States, we were contacted by a young promoter by the name of Martin Lewis, who lived in Hollywood, California. He wanted to promote The Comets, and eventually manage us. Martin had a sense of history, and the year was 2004, the 50th anniversary of the birth of rock 'n' roll.

> …we were enshrined at
> Hollywood's RockWalk, right by the
> Hollywood Walk of Fame. We put our
> handprints in the concrete patio,
> along with our signatures and
> also got a commemorative plaque
> from the mayor of Los Angeles

He had us on CNN with Wolf Blitzer, and we did about 10 minutes live. We performed "Rock Around the Clock" and did an interview, and then we did a show out in Hollywood where we were enshrined at Hollywood's RockWalk, right by the Hollywood Walk of Fame. We put our handprints in the concrete patio, along with our signatures and also got a commemorative plaque from the mayor of Los Angeles.

We did several shows, including *The*

The Original Comets making their hand imprints
in the concrete for Hollywood's Rockwalk

The Original Comets posing with the
finished concrete for Hollywood's RockWalk

The Original Comets with Brenda Lee in Jackson, Tennessee at the Rockabilly Festival, 2000

Early Show with Harry Smith. Then, the jet propulsion laboratory at NASA, located near Los Angeles, was having an event where they were going to shoot a comet out of the sky from a space probe they had launched much earlier. If the space probe shot and hit the comet, it would be a big historic event.

So Martin Lewis had us scheduled to do a show for the jet propulsion laboratory in California to celebrate the success of their shooting the comet with a space probe. It was like finding a needle in a haystack but it actually happened in 2005 during our Fifty

Matt Lucas (blues singer and drummer), Marshall, DJ Fontana (Elvis Presley's original drummer), Dick Richards, Joey Ambrose, Narvel Felts (rockabilly singer and performer)

Years of Rock celebration. So while we were in L.A., The Comets went over to Pasadena and did a show for all those professors and those extremely intelligent people who ran our space administration. And man, we had them out dancing their butts off! We did a show out in a pavilion there and they just had a great time.

In 2005, Martin Lewis wanted us to sign an exclusive contract to give him managerial authority over us. We were not quite ready to make that commitment. He had some grandiose ideas, but we were already content to be doing cruises in the Caribbean.

The first cruise we did was in 2004 with Paul Revere and the Raiders, the Buckinghams, and Gary Puckett and the Union Gap — great organizations, and these people just did wonderful work. In 2005, we did the show with Paul Revere and

Paul Revere

the Raiders (again), Gary Lewis and the Playboys, and Peggy March. In 2006, the Buckinghams returned and Blood, Sweat and Tears appeared.

Paul Revere contacted us because he was starting a new venture in Branson, Missouri and wanted to know what we thought about doing a show there. I had spent several weeks in Branson during the summer of 1992 with Jeanne, and we thought it was one of the greatest places in the United States — shows, entertainment, good weather, big crowds, and a lot of theaters.

Paul Revere said they were opening a new theater and he and Bill Medley of the Righteous Brothers were to be the headliners.

Marshall with one of America's teen idols, Fabian, 2007

He wanted to know if we would be interested in performing as an afternoon show. We said, "Why not, heck yeah, that would be great," so we committed to do our first year at Dick Clark's American Bandstand Theater in Branson. We opened there and our co-star that year was Gary Lewis and the Playboys. Gary Lewis did his hour and then we did ours, with a little break in between shows.

Paul Revere and the Raiders, The Comets, and Gary Lewis were the opening acts, and we alternated weeks. When Paul Revere took a week off, they would bring in Fabian and Bobby Vee, and a show called "The Original Stars of American Bandstand."

Bill Medley is one of the class acts in show business. He lost his singing partner, Bobby Hatfield, in 2003. But Paul Revere's organization hired Bill Medley's son, Darren Medley, as his lead singer. Darren had a career as a businessman and then, three or four years ago, decided suddenly that he would also be in show business. Although he has been a singer only about four years,

Marshall, Dick and Joe at the Dick Clark American
Bandstand Theater in Branson, Missouri, 2008

he is very polished. Darren has rock 'n' roll
blood running in his veins and has become
not only Paul Revere's lead singer but the
partner of his father on the Bill Medley show
where he sings the parts of Bobby Hatfield.

In the second year we did at Dick Clark's
American Bandstand Theater, they brought
in some co-stars to give people a sampling
of the fifties shows. One was the wonderful
personality and voice of David Somerville
of The Diamonds. David has a tremendous

amount of talent and is a class act all the way. David was the lead on "Little Darling," "The Stroll," and "Silhouettes."

When we were on, it was usually with David Somerville in the afternoon. Then when we were off for a week or two, they would bring in Danny and the Juniors to co-star with other acts like Johnny Preston, ("Running Bear"), the lead singer for the Shirelles, and the Crickets (Buddy Holly's band – "That'll Be the Day," "Oh Boy," "Peggy Sue"). We and all the people at Branson loved them.

We were so thrilled and honored to be part of that organization at the Dick Clark American Bandstand Theater. The theater is owned by Glenn Patch, a wonderful

Marshall, singing at Dick Clark's American Bandstand Theater, 2008

Dick Richards, July 2007

man and a wonderful businessman. He is responsible for the new Branson airport that will bring people in from all parts of the world. We won't have to drive back to Springfield to catch a flight back to anywhere. Everyone will just come to us in Branson.

I guess I should backtrack right here and give an update on my personal life from the year 2001. I was in Las Vegas and Jeanne was at home in Florida minding a home furnishing store we had started. We were equal owners, but basically it was her store. I worked there only when I was not on tour.

One day I called home as I usually did every day. I spoke to Jeanne and asked how everything was going. She said "Oh, OK. By the way, I want a divorce."

I had absolutely no inkling that there was a problem with our marriage. I said "What's going on, what is this?" She said "Oh, it has been coming on for a long time." I said "Is there somebody else in your life?" And she said, "No, just want a divorce."

I said "Well, can we talk about it when I get home?" She said "Yes, but that won't help." So I said, "Well would you pick me up at the airport?" She said she would. I was quite upset and all the way home I was trying to figure out what went wrong with my marriage.

When I arrived at the Tampa airport, she met me the way she always did. When we got in the car, she handed me a key and said "This is where your stuff is. I have moved you out, and changed all the locks on the doors of the business and the house. I have put all the properties into my name."

I said "What else?" She said "I have put the titles to the cars in my name, and your stuff is located here." She handed me a key to a storage shed. I was dumbfounded. So I said, "Wow, well can I sleep in the guest bedroom tonight?" She said "Yes, but you will have to move out tomorrow."

I said "You can have the business, but I want the little cash reserve we have put away in the safe."

She wanted a quick divorce. I moved into our motor home and put it in a nearby RV park. It would be my little nest where I could stay between tours. This went on for a number of months.

One day, while making a drive-through deposit at our local bank, this beautiful teller smiled at me and she said "Hi, Tommy, how are you today?" I had never noticed her before, but suddenly I was very taken with her. I went around and parked in the parking lot and went inside the bank to find her. "Are you married?" I asked. She said "No, I'm not." And I said "Would you go to dinner with me tonight?" She thought for a minute and then she said "Well, yes, I will."

So I made arrangements to meet her at

a local restaurant after she got off work. We had a drink and a lovely dinner. And we became the best of friends. I needed someone in my life and I found her. Her name is Cathy Smith. She is the love of my life and we have been extremely close ever since that meeting in November of 2001.

Cathy and Marshall

Last March, just prior to my going on a 20-day concert tour of Europe, my urologist recommended that I have a biopsy done for prostate cancer. I told him to send me an e-mail if he needed to contact me. Two weeks later, I got an e-mail: "Hello, you have prostate cancer. We will fix it when you get back to the States." That was pretty devastating news, but I decided to follow his advice and wait.

When I got home, I went to the doctor and was informed that I needed to get

43 radiation treatments in Springfield, Missouri, which is a full hour from Branson. Given The Comets' schedule, I had to wait until July to start the radiation treatments and got shots in the meantime to keep the cancer under control.

Cathy came up to visit in July, and we did all 43 round trips together. Fortunately, the treatments were completely successful. The cancer is gone for now, and I will be doing 6-month follow-ups to make sure it stays gone.

My life couldn't be better. The Comets have been blessed. Joe and Dick and I are so happy to be able to do what we do in show business. We have also been so lucky to have two of the greatest musicians we have ever hired. David Byrd, our keyboard player, is absolutely the best there is, and our guitar player, Jackson Haney from Borger, Texas, is a lad who keeps us in high spirits at all times. He also happens to play great guitar and sings wonderful songs.

David Byrd is married to Mary Lou

Turner, one of the great country and western singers from the *Grand Ole Opry*. She started her *Grand Ole Opry* career back in the 70's and got very popular, and then became the singing partner of "Whispering Bill" Anderson. They had a lot of wonderful

The Original Comets at Lincoln Center New York City, July 2007

hits together and she still performs in Branson, as part of a show called 'The Grand Ladies of the *Grand Ole Opry*." They perform in one of the local theaters and are one of our favorite shows. We go to see them all the time.

It is such a joy to be able to continue to have my relationship with Cathy. She loves thrill rides. When I took her to Las Vegas back in 2002 (her first visit ever to Las Vegas), we went up on top of the big tower

Marshall, Joey and Jackson
at Lincoln Center in 2007

where they have the roller coaster, on top of the dome, and, figuring that I would ride it with her, I bought two tickets. When I got up on top of that thing, however, I changed my mind. She rode it twice and had a great time, but I did ride the other ones with her, the roller coaster through the hotel/casino New York, New York, and then we went on to ride the other ones around town.

Our 2007 European tour ended in Wolfsburg, Germany, also known as "The Motor City" because it is the home of Volkswagen. They employ 50,000 people and their factory is about five miles long. They make thousands and thousands of cars every day.

Bill Haley Jr. singing with The Original Comets
Gloucester, New Jersey, July 2007

They put us up at a hotel right in the Volkswagen headquarters, a five star Ritz-

Carlton hotel. The promoter had set it up where we were to be treated like stars and we each had our own suite. When we checked in, the people at the desk said "be sure to check your bathroom when you get into your suite."

So we wondered, well, what's the big deal

about checking the bathroom. After checking in, we put our bags in, and looked around, and on the table of the desk, as you walked into the suite, they had a bowl of fruit, and a cake that was made by the local chef. "Welcome Mr. Lytle" was written in chocolate around the dish. I was quite taken by that.

Then I started looking around and I went into the bathroom and there was a freshly drawn bubble bath, in a big claw foot tub, a bottle of cognac, and some chocolates in a tray, sitting next to the bathtub. So, boy oh boy, what an invitation to chill out, and that's exactly what we all did.

We just took our clothes off and jumped in the bathtubs, because we didn't have anything to do for a couple of hours and that was the most relaxing thing we could have done.

Later that afternoon they had a special tour arranged for us of the Volkswagen museum. They drove us to the museum in new Bentleys because Volkswagen company also owns the Bentley automobile company. They sure treated us with class.

After the tour of the facilities and the place where we were going to perform, we did a sound check and we came back and we had that evening off. They had planned a special dinner that would be cooked just for us, by the head chef of the hotel.

We did our show for the people the next day and then the following day we came home from Wolfsburg, Germany back to the United States. Klaus Kettner our manager and friend from Munich, Germany had arranged this entire tour, and it was really, really lovely. This was in 2002 or 2003, and it was wonderful. We still go back and forth to Europe at least once and sometimes twice a year.

The Bill Haley Museum is located in Munich, Germany and it is run and operated by Klaus Kettner, our European manager. He has a lot of memorabilia in the museum. He has been able to acquire some of the gold records from the estate of Billy Williamson. He has

The Original Comets at the
Bill Haley and The Comets Museum
Munich, Germany

Billy's steel guitar and one of my band jackets on display and he has just so much memorabilia. It's really a very interesting museum to go through.

There's a record shop in the front of the museum with over 1,000 albums of Bill Haley. We never recorded that many, but there are what you'd call "bootlegs." The people would take "Rock Around the Clock" and get a bunch of other old obscure songs and make an album out of it and put it on the market and sell it. Bill and the band never made any money off of those bootleg things — that's one of the problems with the record industry. All those little countries over there would just do anything they could to make a buck. Klaus got copies of all these albums, and he's got different CDs and videos and things that people really like to see. He also sells posters from the movies and different shows that we have done. He has kept Bill Haley's name alive

While The Original Comets were on tour in Germany they had a flat tire on the Autobon, and could not fix it. Had to call for help.

in Europe with the fans. The museum opened in 2007 and we were at the grand opening. Every time we go back to Munich we go and make an appearance and he invites fans and the press and whoever he can to come and meet us and talk. It's good P.R.

Another man who became a long-time friend of ours was named Herbert Komits, from Vienna, Austria. Herbert was the world's number one Bill Haley fan and music collector with over 1,000 albums.

Of course, we never recorded that many, but they kept putting them out. As a collector of Bill Haley memorabilia, Herbert Komits was certainly the kingpin of them all. We became very, very close friends with Herbert and his wife, Ermgard, as we did with a lot of other people in the Vienna area, where we still perform to this day.

In 2008, we started in Malaga, Spain, and then we went to Zurich, Switzerland, and then did some other little towns in Germany and Switzerland and then we went to Vienna, Austria. Then we came back and did a couple more shows in Germany, and then back in February to our wonderful, wonderful home base of Branson, Missouri.

Marshall and David Hasselhof at a TV show in Germany, 2005

That is where we were all year in 2008 starting in March through December. Then in January of

2009 we cruised through the Caribbean again, touring with the Harmon Travel Agency. They do these oldies cruises and Paul Revere and the Raiders, Bobby Vee, Fabian and The Comets go cruising through the eastern and western Caribbean.

On February 20, 2009, The Orlando Hard Rock Café invited me to sign my original bass fiddle. I bought that bass fiddle, an Epiphone blond-colored bass, at a music shop in South

Marquee announcing event of signing of Marshall's old bass at The Hard Rock Café, Orlando, Florida, February 2009

Marshall signing the bass
and thanking the crowd
at the Hard Rock event

Marshall's old double bass that he played on
"Rock Around the Clock," now on display
at The Hard Rock Café

Philadelphia for $300. I bought it on time
payments for something like $50 a week
and was able to pay it off quickly.

I eventually sold it through Sotheby's
auction house, but Sotheby's never told me
who bought it. Years later, the bass turned
up at the Hard Rock Café in Orlando, Florida,

where it is displayed on the wall. The Hard Rock Café bought it! I was thrilled when they had me over for a ceremony to sign my bass fiddle. It was quite an honor. And they asked me to get up and sing a few songs.

I was one of the pioneers of the slap bass style. There are literally hundreds of bass players in Europe who play these festivals and they copy everything that I do. I had a meeting with Brian Setzer of the Stray Cats, who had an 18 piece orchestra. He invited me back to his dressing room one time down in Florida. We had a long conversation about where the clicking noise on our recordings came from. He said, "We tried to get that clicking noise beating on tables and barstools and boxes and different things." So I said, "No, it came right off of the bass neck, where the strings would slap against the fingerboard." And he said, "Is that how you got that?" and I said yeah, and I demonstrated it for him, and the next week he had a slap bass player in his orchestra.

In the recording of "Rock Around the Clock" there were two microphones, one on the fingerboard and one on the f-holes of the bass. They cranked it up and you can hear the slap bass — it's very prevalent on the record. It booms right out there at you.

Somewhere around the year 2000, in Paris, France we were doing a show and after our show we had a Meet and Greet autograph

> …it was a picture of me
> with my bass and my signature
> was under the picture,
> tattooed right on his arm.

session and this guy came over and he put his arm on the table, and he said, "Look at that!" And I looked at it and it was a picture of me with my bass and my signature was under the picture, tattooed right on his arm. I said, "Wow, I know how you got the picture but how the heck did you get my signature on your arm?" And he said, "Well, last year when you were here I put my arm out and had you autograph it. Then I went home and had my picture developed, and there's this great picture of you standing on the bass and I said, hell, I'll have that put on there." And I said, "Well why would you do something like that?" And he said, "You don't understand, do you?" I said, "Hell, no." He said, "You're the most copied bass player in the world." I said, "Get out!" And then, I started thinking about that and I guess he was right.

We had a wonderful Oldies Cruise in January, 2009 with Paul Revere and The Raiders, and Bobby Vee and his great family, also the Guess Who, and Dean Torrence of Jan and Dean, plus our good Buddy Jimmy Jay and others. We got to catch up with a lot of old friends, and we made a lot of new friends who came along. Nice ship, the MSC Orchestra (passenger capacity over 3,000).

Comets cruising with Paul Revere, Bobby Vee,
The Guess Who and Dean Torrence of Jan and Dean

A little crowded, but we all had a great time.

When we docked, The Original Comets caught a flight to Des Moines, Iowa, for the 50th anniversary commemoration of "The Day the Music Died," the plane crash killing Buddy Holly, Ritchie Valens and "The Big Bopper" in 1959. The weather was about 4 degrees with blowing snow. We stayed in a hotel for a couple of days before our hotel in Clearlake, was ready. When we arrived it was about 12 below, just too cold for me. On Wednesday night we went to the Surf

Ballroom to check it out and see what was going on. The doors opened at 6:30 PM and the ballroom filled up with wall-to-wall people.

Dick, Terry Stewart (President of Rock and Roll Hall of Fame), Marshall, Joey

Every show every night was sold out. Our friend Terry Stewart, the President of the Rock and Roll Hall of Fame in Cleveland had a table and invited us to sit with them.

Marshall and Elena Holly (Buddy's widow)

I sat next to Maria Elena Holly (Buddy's widow) and Ritchie Valens' sister, Connie. There was some great entertainment that opening night. The Original White Sidewalls was the first group and they were very, very good. The headliner that night was Jason D. Williams, who does a similar act to Jerry Lee Lewis, with 10 times the energy. It was his 50th birthday. They loved him and he gave them his all and hit a home run. The next night, Thursday January 29th, the show was started off by Tommy Allsup (Buddy Holly's guitar player the night of the fatal crash) and Johnny Rogers sang some of Buddy Holly's hits. The Host and emcee for the night was our buddy Dave Somerville of The Diamonds. He did some of The Diamonds hits and a little Fats Domino, and some Buddy Holly songs. He is always good. Then came Dodie Stevens who had a big hit with "Pink Shoe Laces." She did about 20 minutes, and the crowd loved her. Then another nostalgia group The Tymes did about 30 minutes of some great harmony. Then Johnny Tillotson came on and sang some great songs and some of his hits and the audience loved him.

We did our regular show that ran a little over an hour. The crowd rewarded us with thunderous applause. The shows were over for that night. The Comets went to the Meet and Greet table to shake hands with some of our fans and sign autographs.

February 3, 2009
Graham Nash holding his ticket stub
to a Bill Haley and The Comets concert
he attended in the fifties

Graham Nash was at the event. He posed for a photo of himself in which he is holding up a ticket stub from a Bill Haley and The Comets concert. He attended the concert back in the fifties and carries the sticket stub in his wallet to this day.

In March we started our European Tour with Klaus Kettner, and we returned in April to our homes in Branson, Missouri and opened our new season at the Andy Williams Moon River Theatre. I hope you all can come visit us in Branson some time soon. Our new airport opened for business in May 2009.

We just have the time of our lives. That's a song Bill Medley recorded that was in the movie "Dirty Dancing." The time of my life. That's the way we feel right now. We are having the time of our lives. We're very lucky to be loved and adored by a lot of wonderful people and we're going to keep doing this as long as the Good Lord allows us to.

Dick is having his 85th birthday in 2009, Joey will be having his 75th birthday, and I will be having my 76th birthday.

Gutarist Franny Beecher became 85 years old while we were playing in Branson, Missouri. Franny Beecher was kind of a lonely person and he really missed his family and when we'd have a week or two off he'd go back home and not want to come back. He's now retired.

Johnny Grande got very ill and passed on in June of 2006.

Mary Wilson of The
Supremes and Marshall

The Lennon Sisters, Marshall
and singer Larry Gatlin of
the Gatlin Brothers in Branson

Freddie Cannon (singer
of many hits in the 50s
and 60s), with Marshall
in Branson at a Show
called "Bowzer's Rock 'n'
Roll Party"

May 2009, Branson, Missouri
The Original Comets and
Kathy and Janet Lennon of
the Lennon Sisters

Bowzer with The Original Comets

Billy Williamson passed away in 1996 and he was kind of a recluse and gave up show business when he and Bill Haley split up. He vowed that he would never talk about show business or Bill Haley or ever tell anybody that he was ever associated with Bill Haley and The Comets.

And now I'm branching out into acting. A recent development for me is that Bertie Higgins, recording artist, film producer, and president of Cayo Largo Productions, in Burbank, California, has signed me to do a featured role in his new film production entitled *Through the Eye* to be filmed in Tarpon Springs, Florida in the Fall of 2009. The story deals with drugs being smuggled into the Gulf coast of Florida from Colombia, South America during the mid 1970s. I'm so excited to be acting in this film.

So, you all, I hope that you enjoyed this book and I hope you enjoyed this story about this old rock 'n' roller who won't give up. Y'all take care now. God Bless.

"Doing something is better
than doing nothing
because if you're doing nothing,
you'll never know
when you're finished."

— *Marshall Lytle*